THE DEVELOPMENT OF THE IRISH TOWN

THE DEVELOPMENT
OF THE IRISH TOWN

Edited by R.A. BUTLIN

CROOM HELM LONDON

ROWMAN AND LITTLEFIELD TOTOWA N.J.

© 1977, Preface, 'Urban and Proto-Urban Settlements in Pre-Norman Ireland',
  'Irish Towns in the Sixteenth and Seventeenth Century', R.A. Butlin

© 1977, 'The Towns of Medieval Ireland', B.J. Graham

© 1977, 'Irish Towns in the Eighteenth and Nineteenth Centuries' T.W. Freeman

Croom Helm Ltd, 2-10 St John's Road, London SW11

ISBN 0-85664-489-7

First published in the United States 1977 by
Rowman and Littlefield, Totowa, New Jersey

ISBN 0-87471-979-8

F11

Printed in Great Britain
by Redwood Burn Ltd, Trowbridge and Esher

CONTENTS

PREFACE

Ireland is not a highly urbanised island in comparison with her West European neighbours, but none the less has a long history of urban development stretching back in all probability into prehistory, and intensifying during the medieval Norman colonisation and settlement, the period of Tudor and Stuart plantations, and in the eighteenth and nineteenth centuries. The ground evidence for the study of urban history and development is plentiful, and recent urban site excavations, notably those in Dublin, have provided more grist for the intellectual mill. The documentary evidence is not particularly wealthy, but there is sufficient to work on. It is strange, therefore, that so little attention should hitherto have been given to the towns and cities of Ireland and their historical evolution, for the potential for studies of individual towns, of the Irish urban system as a whole, and for comparative studies with urban systems and development elsewhere, is great. Such important and significant works as G. Camblin's *The Town in Ulster* (1951), Constantia Maxwell's *Country and Town in Ireland under the Georges* (1940), and *Dublin under the Georges* (revised 1956), J.J. Webb's *Municipal Government in Ireland* (1918), M. Craig's *Dublin, 1660-1860* (1952), the collective work edited by J.C. Beckett and R.E. Glasscock on *Belfast* (1967), and the urban sections of such works as E. MacLysaght's *Irish Life in the Seventeenth Century* (1950) and T.W. Freeman's *Pre-Famine Ireland* (1957) could and should have been mirrored in a host of additional books and monographs, but we are still too heavily dependent in studies of urbanisation in Ireland on the heavily antiquarian studies of individual towns produced in the nineteenth century.

While the study of historical urban development (or decline) is the prerogative of no one discipline, it is a subject which has attracted the attentions of geographers in the past and continues to do so at the present. The three contributors to this short volume are all geographers, of differing approaches and interests, but linked by a common interest in Ireland and its historical geography. This work is not a fully comprehensive statement on the detailed history and historical geography of urbanisation in Ireland. Its basic purpose is to review urbanisation in Ireland down to the end of the nineteenth century and to function, where deemed appropriate, as a stimulus to and foundation for more elaborate and extensive studies of this particular subject.

R.A. Butlin

Queen Mary College, University of London
November 1976

ACKNOWLEDGEMENTS

The editor wishes to acknowledge the invaluable assistance of the secretarial and cartographic staff of the Geography Department, Queen Mary College, University of London, and also the comments and suggestions kindly made by Professor V.B. Proudfoot and Dr R.E. Glasscock on preliminary drafts of Chapter 1. The Board of Trinity College, Dublin, have kindly given permission for the reproduction of MS 1209 ('Hardiman atlas') nos. 42 and 64. Permission to base Figures 13 and 14 and 16-19 on maps first published in *Pre-Famine Ireland* (1957) was granted by Manchester University Press. Figure 15 is reproduced by kind permission of George L. Davies from *Irish Geography*, Vol. 2, No. 3 (1951).

1 URBAN AND PROTO—URBAN SETTLEMENTS IN PRE-NORMAN IRELAND

R.A. Butlin

Introduction

The weight of opinion in most works on early and medieval Ireland favours a Norman origin for the earliest substantial wave of urbanism in Ireland, prefaced by a small number of Viking settlements. Binchy, for example, states that 'urban civilisation . . . remained quite foreign to the Celtic-speaking peoples of these islands until it was more or less imposed on them by foreign conquerors,'[1] and Chadwick discounts, on the evidence of the early Irish laws, 'the existence in early medieval Wales or Ireland of town or communal life'.[2] Of fifth-century Ireland, the de Paors write that 'The economy of this society was pastoral and agricultural. There were no cities or towns,'[3] and Jones Hughes, in the only comprehensive paper to date on Irish urban origins, asserts that 'the essentially rural culture of Ireland, like that of the Balkans, had crystallised before the introduction of towns by aliens.'[4] Expressed in more hypothetical terms, the general theory thus induced from the study of archaeological, literary and legendary evidence is one of secondary urban generation resulting from primary diffusion of urban form and organisation.[5] Such a hypothesis may be partially substantiated with reference to the evidence of early urban charters, the limited records of urban government, 'relict' features of morphology and findings from excavations.

Debates on urban origins, however, have an interesting tendency to change course from time to time in relation to new ideas or concepts of urbanism and the discovery of new evidence. Thus, in recent years the debate on English urban origins has been conclusively resolved in favour of the 'Taitians' or pre-Norman Conquest urbanisation advocates, for there is now

a growing sense of wonder that scholars could ever seriously have held that the Anglo-Saxons, outside London, had no town worthy of the name. From Alfred's establishment of burhs and the work of his children, Edward and Aethelflaed, through the plentiful diplomatic, legal, and ancillary material of the tenth and early eleventh centuries to the great storehouse of Domesday Book, there is

evidence enough for the existence of towns, and firm and conclusive
indication of varied and subtly complex urban growth . . . Work on
coinage alone, with all its bearing on urbanisation, has been enough
to establish the existence of towns beyond all reasonable doubt.[6]

Ireland, of course, had no Anglo-Saxon colonisation, but it is becoming
increasingly hard, in the face of evidence from other regions of Dark
Age Europe suggesting early forms of urban life or pre-urban nuclei, to
continue to exempt Ireland from the processes of change in the
settlement system leading towards fixed urban forms of settlement.
Many instances of settlement change were, as we shall see, short-lived
and atrophied by historical circumstance, so that a logical progression
along a settlement evolution pattern was thwarted or truncated. None
the less, if urbanism be conceived as a way of life, or attitude of mind,
and is associated with the significant presence of non-primary produc-
ing occupations and functions, the evidence for Ireland is worthy of
review in the context of the possibility of a 'spontaneous readjustment
of social, political and economic relationships within the context of a
folk society',[7] that is, an examination of the possibility of the existence
of some form or forms of urban society in Ireland prior to the Norman
colonisation of the twelfth century and of the significance of pre-urban
or proto-urban sites which may have acted as foci for later urban settlements.

One major theoretical, semantic and operational problem in this
context is the interpretation and connotation given to such ambiguous
and omnibus terms as 'urban' and 'urbanism'. In terms of pre-industrial
urban settlement, the plethora of modern writing on urbanisation in
the nineteenth century and beyond is of little help. More relevant is
the work of such specialists on early urban development and the processes of change in peasant societies such as Sjoberg,[8] Wheatley[9] and
Redfield,[10] and, perhaps, in a broader context, the work of Harvey.[11]
Sjoberg's observations and assertions on the pre-industrial city have
direct relevance to the towns and cities of medieval Ireland.[12]
Wheatley's ideas on nuclear urbanism, his ceremonial-centre-origin
theory for the beginnings of urban form, taken together with Redfield's
concept of the folk-urban continuum, provide a liberal conceptual
framework within which Irish urban and proto-urban forms may be
considered. For purpose of this essay the term 'urban' will be used not
only in relation to a physically distinctive entity with a relatively large
population and redistributive functions, but also in relation to settlements whose function and inhabitants exhibit traits, be they cultural,

religious, administrative or ceremonial, sufficiently distinctive to distinguish them from predominantly 'rural' forms of settlement and occupation. This ambivalent connotation has the advantage of allowing a more flexible review of the evidence than has been attempted hitherto and, perhaps, of stimulating further debate of a question much in need of further exploration.

Viking Towns

The Viking invasions of Ireland which began in the eighth century have long been regarded as disruptive to the somewhat stagnant calm of early Irish society. Thus a twelfth-century account claims that it was not possible to

> recount, or narrate, or enumerate, or tell, what all the Irish suffered in common, both men and women, laity and clergy, old and young, noble and ignoble, of hardship and of injury, and of oppression, in every house, from these valiant, wrathful, foreign, purely-pagan people.[13]

The Vikings were undoubtedly avid and effective plunderers, bent on acquiring silverware and other valuables, food, corn, armour (such commodities having frequently been stored in monasteries for safe keeping) and slaves. The earliest Viking raid was in 795 when Lambay Island (near Dublin) was invaded, and the raids increased in intensity with the arrival of Turgeis in 830. The monastic annalists, on whose accounts we largely rely for evidence of Viking activity, maximised their disruptive effects, and the general picture they paint is one of almost universal destruction. Recent commentaries suggest, however, that the Vikings were no more culpable in respect of the burning and pillaging of churches and monasteries than were the Irish themselves, the latter over a much longer period of time,[14] and that the changes effected by this new culture had some positive merit, notably in the form of the introduction of coinage and of towns. In the mid-ninth century the Viking raiders began to establish permanent harbours and settlements around the coast of Ireland: it appears that at the end of the tenth century, having suffered a series of defeats, they turned their attentions more closely to trading, a change 'symbolised by the beginning of a Dublin coinage in about 955'.[15] The warships and supply ships used in the ninth century were very much larger than those used in the earliest raids, and could not simply be run up on to beaches, as before, as 'landing craft'.[16] Dams were constructed to hold back sufficient water for the larger ships, and the resulting fortified ship harbour was known in Irish as a *longphort*. Such *longphorts* were constructed in many places, including Dublin, Waterford, Wexford, Cork, Youghal and Limerick, and were frequently attacked by the Irish. The *Annals of Ulster*, for example, record that in '866 Aed, King of Cenel Eogain and Ui Neill overlord plundered all the longphorts where the Vikings had settled along the coast of north-east Ireland, carrying off spoils and flocks and herds'.[17]

The development of the *longphorts* obviously rendered the Vikings more vulnerable to attack than before when their bases were not fixed, and both major and minor sites suffered as a consequence. The settlement at Dublin constructed about 841 AD, for example, was severely ravaged in 847 and 849, and the new settlement at Cork was destroyed in 848. The Norsemen also suffered from Danish attacks: in 851 a fleet of Danish ships attacked Dublin.[18] Notwithstanding their turbulent history, several of the new defended ship harbours developed as trading settlements, including those which are now the largest coastal cities of Ireland (except for Belfast). The larger trading vessels developed at this time facilitated a gradual expansion of trade between Ireland and Scandinavia in such commodities as wine, textiles, luxury goods and slaves. The Norse sagas refer to Dublin as an important trading town, and records of goods seized in an Irish raid on Limerick indicate their European and Eastern origins. O'Corráin has indicated the significance of linguistic evidence for Norse trade:

> The Irish words *margad* 'a market', *mangaire* 'a dealer', *marg* 'a mark' and *pingin* 'a penny', as well as a host of other words connected directly or indirectly with trade or shipping, derive from Old Norse. The haggling of the merchants is referred to in another text as *gioc-goc* or broken speech of the Norse dealers.[19]

The coin and coin hoard evidence also enhances the significance of Dublin as a principal city and trading centre. Before about 995 the coins used in Ireland were mainly English, but in about 995 with the beginning of the Dublin mint new coins were struck: Hiberno-Norse/Danish style coins which were imitative copies of English coins. From 1000 onwards there are two coin series: 'First there are imitations of contemporary Anglo-Saxon coins, ending with some copies of coins of Cnut . . . The second series consists of Dublin copies of its own coins, struck on extremely thin flans.'[20] It appears that one of the purposes of coin-making was to facilitate trade with Anglo-Saxon England.

The dominance of Dublin among the seaboard towns is shown by the high proportion of coin hoards found in its vicinity. Until recently, very little was known of the form of the Irish Viking towns, except by conjectural analogy with such Baltic trading settlements as Haithabu-Sliaswik near Schleswig, and Birka in Sweden. Excavations at Haithabu since 1900 have revealed a fortified town with narrow streets, with wooden and wattle houses, and a canalised stream. Finds from the town include a wide range of artefacts, varying from carvings from bone, wood and amber to more sophisticated products.[21]

A realistic comparison between the Viking settlements in Ireland and those elsewhere is now possible as a result of the highly important excavations in Dublin in the last few years,[22] for the High Street and Winetavern Street excavations have provided a great deal of new evidence. The Viking settlement on a low hill on the south bank of the River Liffey covered an area of approximately 775 square metres, within the area of the subsequent medieval town walls. The base of the site was boulder clay (not peat, as hitherto imagined, the latter being organic refuse from the town). Many of the houses had been constructed by a post-and-wattle technique (the walls comprising horizontal rods of hazel, ash, and elm interlaced with upright posts, forming a wickerwork which was covered with clay daub), and others were constructed from squared timbers. A number of significant finds indicate the origins and functions of the settlement. One of these is the outline of a Viking ship scratched on a plank. Other finds indicate trades and crafts similar to those performed in Viking settlements elsewhere: the finds include a gilt-bronze disc brooch, probably of tenth-century date and similar to one found at Birka, soapstone moulds for casting silver ingots, lead weights, bone combs, bronze and iron pins, padlocks and keys, gold armlets and coins. This material is similar to that found in Viking sites in Scandinavia and Germany, and further excavation in Dublin and other *longphort* sites will undoubtedly reveal further similarities of form and function.

The significance of the Viking settlements in Ireland was recognised by the Normans, who gave them, with the exception of Wexford, the status of 'royal' towns. Dublin, for example, was granted a charter and the 'liberties of the men of Bristol' in 1171, and similar charters were later granted to Waterford, Cork and Limerick. After the Norman conquest the fate of the Norse inhabitants of the major towns varied, but many of them lived in clearly identified Norse 'quarters', such as Oxmantown in Dublin.[23]

The social, economic and political context within which this urban development took place is of interest. The period of the ninth and tenth centuries was undoubtedly a time of change in Ireland, during which some old 'taboos' were abandoned (in pre-Viking warfare 'territory was normally not annexed, nor were lands confiscated, tribal dynasties were not de-throned, neutral zones were usually observed'[24]), church property lost its status of neutrality, development in ecclesi-astical and secular law terminated, a revolution in land ownership began, development of over-lordship took place and some powerful monastic *paruchiae* began to emerge.[25] It can be argued that this matrix of changes was in large measure triggered off by the Viking depradations, which also added an urban dimension by creating ship harbours which developed into trading settlements. The relationship between these changes and urban development may be expressed perhaps in terms of stimulus innovation, for the Viking activities encouraged the polarisa-tion of political authority — as a matter of strategic necessity — and the emulation by the Irish of their seafaring abilities (extended use of ships by the Irish in the tenth century is a noticeable trait), trading activities and urban bases. Evidence of the latter relates to Irish dominance of those 'new' towns in the eleventh and twelfth centuries and the establish-ment of royal residences in the towns in the twelfth century.[26] It is interesting to note that the society affected by changes stimulated by the Vikings was, in many respects, similar in character to that of pre-Christian Scandinavia,[27] and also to speculate on the effects of coastal town development on any incipient urban development in the interior of Ireland One line of argument suggests that if earliest town develop-ment in Ireland was the result of an earlier stimulus, that is the intro-duction of Christianity, then Norse activities may well have arrested town growth other than at their own coastal ports.[28] It seems more likely however, albeit in more hypothetical terms, that Norse coastal urban development would have enhanced the development of interior 'central places' of low order through the development of major peri-pheral nodes of a new 'central place' system, for Norse fortification of Ireland's external trading contacts would have required an active supply hinterland with some nodal points for each of the major ports.

Ireland before the Vikings: Pre-Urban Nuclei and the Beginnings of Urbanism

What evidence is there for incipient urban development in Ireland before the Viking settlements were established, and to what extent was such development accelerated or truncated in the course of time? The

evidence is extremely scanty, but it is possible and necessary to postu-
late and consider the existence of a variety of proto-urban forms in the
light of the experience of other regions of Western Europe. Much of
Western Europe in late pre-historic and early historic time, including
some of the areas colonised by Celtic-speaking peoples, had proto-
urban forms of settlement. Thus the *oppida* of Celtic peoples, frequently mentioned by Caesar, were essentially fortresses, primitive
refuges which may once have been no more than temporarily occupied
but which were increasingly becoming permanent centres of trade,
crafts, administration and religion in the more developed parts of
Gaul'.[29] The extent to which such features subsequently became
important urban settlements varied, but the fact has certainly been
recognised for Western Europe and for England. It is strange, and somewhat paradoxical, therefore, that little consideration has been given to
the Irish equivalents of the *oppida* — the hill-forts — or to other pre-
Norman settlements which functioned as central places and were
centres of economic, social and administrative activities. If the
'imported urbanisation' thesis has not been extensively used in explanation of urban origins in other parts of Western Europe, it seems strange
that it should still prevail in respect of Irish urban origins. It might perhaps be argued that Ireland's peripheral position at the 'Atlantic ends'
of Europe would mitigate against even 'imported urbanisation' for a
long period of time, but the extensive contacts of early Christian
Ireland with Europe, through both ecclesiastical links and trade links,
and the activities of Irish pirates in the Irish Sea as early as the fifth
century would negate any such 'isolationist' thesis.

Ireland in the early historic period undoubtedly retained many
characteristics of an Iron Age culture, existing in 'a backwater undis-
turbed by the mainstream of the Latin middle ages'.[30] Early Irish
society was 'tribal, rural, hierarchical and familiar',[31] a description
which evokes a picture of a people retaining their Celtic culture and
polity, unaffected by the dream of Agricola — who thought of con-
quering Ireland with a single legion but (sensibly) changed his mind.
The basic unit of settlement was the fortified *rath* or ring-fort, the
farmstead of the free farmer, though there was probably another type
of settlement, sometimes termed a 'proto-clachan', comprising a loose
cluster of the huts of bondmen. Raths were particularly numerous in
Ireland — nearly forty thousand have been identified — and although
most of them are fairly small in diameter and contain only a single
farmstead, raths of superior quality and size have been identified which
were probably the residences of aristocrats and kings.

The question to be posed at this stage relates to the possibility of the more 'superior' rath acting as some kind of pre-urban nucleus or, indeed, whether some of the royal raths or sites could be defined as urban forms. The answer can only be tentative, for the question is complex for a variety of reasons, including the length of time during which rath-building and occupation took place (estimated at some 1,500 years), the problem of grading raths into some kind of hierarchy, and the difficulty of measuring the significance of the locational coincidence of raths and present-day urban areas.

The case for the direct influence of these larger raths on subsequent urban development has been made strongly for the towns of Ulster by Camblin,[32] who says that many Ulster towns are built on rath sites, arguing that this locational coincidence is probably due to the choice of sites in fertile areas, good strategic sites (proximity to road systems and hill-top locations), citing Dungannon (Gannon's fort or *dun*) and Rathfriland as obvious examples. A careful analysis of the relationship between rath sites and later urban sites for Ireland as a whole would undoubtedly reveal many more coincidental locations, but until more detailed investigation is carried out, both of a statistical and documen-tary nature, the extent and significance of such coincidences cannot be fully tested.

The Irish equivalents of the continental Celtic *oppida* are the hill-forts, structures which are more complicated functionally and mor-phologically than the more numerous and ubiquitous raths. The Irish hill-forts have not been intensively studied in the past, but in recent years more attention has been paid to their typology and function.[33] Three main classes of hill-fort have been suggested by Raftery: those with simple univallate sites, sites with widely spaced multivallate defences, notably hill-top and cliff-top sites; and small inland promon-tory forts.[34] Among the univallate sites are the fort on Cathedral Hill, Downpatrick, and that at Freestone Hill, Co. Kilkenny, and a number of sites which functioned not only as places of defence, but also for assemblies and religious ceremonies, including the major royal sites of Rath na Riogh (Tara, Co. Meath), Emain Macha (Navan Fort, Co. Armagh) and Dun Ailinne (Knockaulin, Co. Kildare). In addition to the major royal sites there are many other minor sites which functioned as centres for tribal kingdoms, for in the period from the fifth to the twelfth century there were large numbers of tribal kingdoms, there being probably no less than 150 'kings' at any time.[35] The size of the forts of these kings varied, but an eighth-century law tract describes their size as being proportionate to the number of base clients who had built it:

> What is the proper fortress for a king who is in constant residence at
> the head of his *tuath*? Seven score feet of full measure the size of his
> fortress in every direction. Seven feet the width of its ditch; twelve
> feet its depth. It is then that he is king when ramparts of base
> clientship surround him. What is the rampart of base clientship,
> Twelve feet the width of its opening and its base and its distance
> from the fortress. Thirty feet its length on the outside.[36]

The larger royal sites generally exhibit an impressive continuity of site
occupation from Neolithic times onwards, and the question arises
whether they could have been in any sense prehistoric central places or
proto-towns? Raftery's comments are pertinent and intriguing in this
context: in his preliminary observations on hill-forts he suggests that
'It seems probable that most of the hill-forts constituted settlements of
quite considerable size, but there seems little, if any, evidence that they
ever achieved the status of towns,'[37] without making clear what 'the
status of towns' was. Later, discussing the univallate royal sites, he
states:

> It seems clear that at Tara, at least, the site was from earliest times
> one of extreme religious significance and it is probably that this
> veneration continued unbroken, and, indeed probably increased, in
> the Iron Age. This may well be the case at Emain Macha and Dun
> Ailinne also. Whether these places became the sites of actual settle-
> ments on any large scale as well is a matter of conjecture. The
> *Dindshencas*, which devotes four lengthy poems to Tara, refers to
> great numbers of houses and legions of warriors existing within the
> ramparts. This may, of course, be dismissed almost completely as
> poetic licence, written some considerable time after the site had
> fallen into disuse; there may, however, be a dim folk memory
> embodied in the exaggerated descriptions, recalling great numbers
> of people dwelling within the defences.[38]

A translation of the Martyrology of Oengus the Culdee, written *c*.
800 AD, interestingly uses the term 'burgh' in connection with the
royal hill-forts: 'Aillen's proud burgh has perished with its warlike host
. . . Emain's burgh it hath vanished, save that the stones remain. . .'[39],
and while this again may be little more than poetic licence, the imagery
is interesting in the context of this discussion of the role and status of

hill-fort settlements in the general settlement hierarchy. There are some fifty hill-forts known in Ireland, of which about twenty are univallate and fifteen have widely spaced multivallate defences; only a small number are of the inland promontory or multivallate closely spaced variety. The forts date variously in origins from at least the Iron Age to the fourth century, and the actual occupation of the sites stretches in some cases from the Neolithic to the twelfth century AD. The first two classes of fort are almost mutually exclusive in distribution.[41]

It is virtually impossible to demonstrate, with the exception of such a case as Downpatrick, a continuity from proto-urban to urban functions on the hill fort sites, for they do represent an historical settlement fault-line or discontinuity, promoted perhaps by the strengthening influence of Christianity in the early Middle Ages in Ireland. None the less, as more material comes to light from excavations, it will be interesting to assess their significance as possible pre-historic/early historic 'central places' or proto-towns.

Monastic Settlements

In pre-Norman Ireland the other forms of settlement which achieved widespread distribution were those resulting from the spread of Christianity, which began with the arrival of St Patrick, who is said to have landed in 432. In the immediate post-Patrician period (the late fifth century) the work of the church was effected by a 'first order' generation, whose leaders were bishops, operating in twelve territorial sees. The concept of a see was derived from the concept of the *civitas* of Roman Europe, based on towns, but in Ireland there were no urban bases as such for the new sees, and the inhabited raths and royal sites were generally inappropriate, though in time the rath sites and some donated royal sites served as bases or models for monastic settlements. In the late fifth century, however, the sees related to the main kingdoms. The bishops, who had much contact with the Irish kings, appeared as 'new-style druids or wizards'[42] to the Irish. In addition to the bishops there were some monasteries and a few hermitages. Although certain monastic houses were founded in the sixth century, such as those at Durrow, Derry, Bangor, Clonmacnois, Clonard, and Clonfert, it was the seventh and eighth centuries that witnessed the massive expansion of monastic settlements, and a 'second order' ecclesiastical generation developed, with 'few bishops and many priests, when large and small monasteries were established in great numbers, and many tens of thousands of Irishmen left their homes to join them'.[43] The extent of the spatial distribution of these monastic

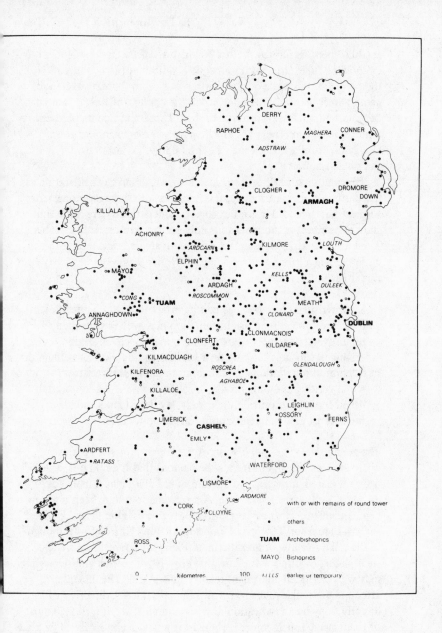

with or with remains of round tower

others

TUAM Archbishoprics

MAYO Bishoprics

KELLS earlier or temporary

0 ___ kilometres ___ 100

Figure 1: Early Celtic Christian Sites

establishments is impressive, though analysis of the maps (Figures 1 and
2) showing their distribution must be conditioned, as with the raths, by
the fact that they were of many different sizes and orders of importance. This is particularly important in the context of their potential
as pre-urban nuclei or proto-urban sites. Those settlements sited on
remote islands and rocks for ascetic purposes, for example, must
clearly be dismissed from such a consideration, as also must many of
the smaller houses.

The larger monastic settlements, however, deserve consideration as
quasi-urban forms or urban nodes. Accounts of the larger monasteries
suggest that, in addition to the religious orders there were quite substantial numbers of students and probably lay farmers and craftsmen.
The term monastic *civitates* has been used, albeit inaccurately, to describe the larger monastic communities. Norman and St Joseph have put
this situation very clearly.

> Later writings describe huge communities with thousands of mem-
> bers, and though monkish imagination may well have tended to
> pious overstatement, the growth of monastic 'cities' around the
> original enclosures suggests very substantial populations at the more
> celebrated foundations. As the monasteries became centres for
> metalworking and other crafts, specialist workers no doubt estab-
> lished themselves outside their walls; lay dependants and clients of
> the monasteries frequently built huts there too.[44]

The actual size of the population of the larger monastic centres is
difficult to establish, but it must be obvious that it could not, as has
been suggested, have reached a figure of *c.* 2,000. Places like Clonmacnois, Kells and Glendalough, for example, can have been nowhere
near equivalent status to the third-rank towns of 'Domesday' England
such as Canterbury, Oxford, Cambridge or Bury St Edmunds, though
in the relatively low-order settlement hierarchy of medieval Ireland
such places, together with Durrow, Ferns, Downpatrick and Armagh
may well have held equivalent relative rank status. The increased
attempts of secular rulers to control the settlements, directly or indirectly, may be an indication of their economic wealth, though most
of them evaded such control. There is, it would seem, a case to be made
for regarding the largest of the monasteries as constituting some form
of town. The form or morphology of these settlements varied, but a
key feature was often a circular enclosure, which may have been a
former rath or a copy of one. Within the enclosure were located the

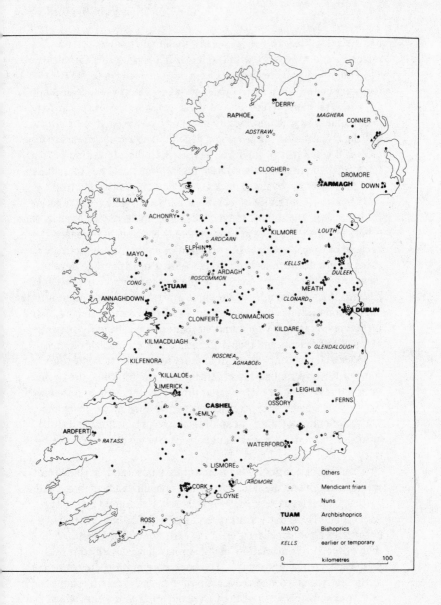

Figure 2: Medieval Monastic Settlements

church or churches, the monks' cells, the library and scriptorium, refectory and workshop, with the farm buildings outside the enclosure. The earlier monastic settlements have been likened (in form) to 'a modern holiday-camp with rows of wooden chalets grouped around a few central halls'.[45] The sites of the larger monasteries appear to have been influenced in some cases by proximity to the larger native forts, but the monasteries' influence and general significance appears to have increased while that of the forts decreased, so that some kind of transference of function appears to have taken place. In some cases, like that of Cashel, sites of royal residences were actually transferred to the church, giving continuity of site use and, to a degree, of site function. In other cases, the sites of some of the larger monastic settlements were ultimately abandoned, as at Clonard and Glendalough, probably because of their locations. The question of continuity of monastic site use is an interesting one, both in the context of Irish urban development and in the broader context of the development of the settlement pattern. Brian Graham has made some interesting investigations into the use of monastic sites by the Norman invaders in eastern Ireland,[46] and further investigations would undoubtedly reveal continuity between Norman settlements and monastic, rath, and even prehistoric sites.

In general terms, therefore, it appears reasonable to conjecture that some of the larger monastic settlements not only fulfilled urban functions but also acted as foci for later urban development, and that even some of the smaller sites acted as foci for Norman urban development. The exact nature of these urban or quasi-urban functions and the influence of monastic pre-urban nuclei clearly needs further investigation.

The case for continuity between ecclesiastical (and, in some cases secular) settlement and later urban development can be demonstrated by such examples as Armagh, Downpatrick, Kells, and Cashel. The Armagh and Downpatrick sites are of particular interest. Armagh did not receive an urban charter until the early seventeenth century, at the time of the Ulster plantation, and historians have described it as an 'Irish ecclesiastical borough'.[47] The impressive hill-top site of the core of the city was chosen as the location for an early church established by St Patrick, but this was not the first occupation of the site, which had a rath on it. The rath, known as Daire's rath, was a secular site, named in the pre-Christian era after the pagan goddess Macha (Ard Macha = Armagh), whose name was also used in the major fort at Navan (Emain Macha) which had been the ceremonial centre, and possibly a residence, of the kings of Ulster.[48] Radio-carbon dating of the ditch round the hill-top at Armagh suggests that it had been created by *c*. 290 AD, and had become a town of some importance: in a raid in 996, some 2,000 cows were taken by the Airgialla; in 1090 nearly one hundred houses were burned; in 1112 three streets were burned and a similar conflagration took place in 1166.[49] Armagh thus represents an extremely interesting example of settlement continuity and of a monastic town. The rath is a distinctive element in the present-day town plan, indicating the secular origins of the site. Downpatrick, similarly, has its cathedral located within a hill-fort on Cathedral Hill, and excavation in various parts has suggested a continuous occupation from the late Bronze Age to the thirteenth or fourteenth century, again involving the use of an earlier site for an important monastic settlement, around which a town grew up.[50]

Conclusion

While recognising that the legally constituted and tenurially different towns of the Norman colonisation constitute an institutional and morphological innovation in Ireland, it is perhaps wrong to suggest that nothing approaching urban status or function had preceded them. The evidence presented above, albeit in a highly conjectural framework, suggests the strong possibility, in addition to the Viking port towns, that some form of central place or proto-urban settlements had developed. Thus the 'imported urbanism only' thesis is inadequate, and needs further critical examination in the light of fresh evidence, for it does not take sufficient cognisance of the effects of social, economic, religious and political changes which were undoubtedly being experienced in the period from the fifth to the twelfth century, and which resulted in the rise of new forms of social organisation and settlement, and, at the other extreme, the demise and redundancy of some features of political and economic organisation which had survived, in all probability, since the Iron Age. The effects of this matrix of changes on settlement forms is still far from clear, but it does seem that in the period under consideration some form of actual or incipient urbanism took place, providing, in some instances, a basis for the more dramatic and sweeping urban development which followed the Norman colonisation.

Notes

1. D.A. Binchy, 'Secular Institutions', in M. Dillon (ed.), *Early Irish Society*

        (1954), p. 55.
 2.   Nora Chadwick, *The Celts* (1970), p. 122.
 3.   L. and M. de Paor, *Early Christian Ireland* (1958), p. 32.
 4.   T. Jones Hughes, 'The Origin and Growth of Towns in Ireland', *University Review*, II (7) (1959), p. 9.
 5.   Paul Wheatley, *The Pivot of the Four Quarters* (1971), p. 6.
 6.   Henry Loyn, 'Towns in late Anglo-Saxon England: the evidence and some possible lines of enquiry', in Peter Clemoes and Kathleen Hughes (eds.), *England Before the Conquest. Studies in Primary Sources presented to Dorothy Whitelock* (1971), pp. 115-16.
 7.   Paul Wheatley, 'Proleptic Observations on the Origins of Urbanism', in R.W. Steel and R. Lawton (eds.), *Liverpool Essays in Geography* (1967), p. 318.
 8.   Gideon Sjoberg, *The Pre-industrial City* (1960); 'The Origin and Evolution of Cities', *Scientific American*, 213 (1965), pp. 55-63.
 9.   Wheatley, *Pivot of the Four Quarters*; 'The concept of urbanism', in P.J. Ucko, R. Tringham and G.W. Dimbleby (eds.), *Man, Settlement and Urbanism* (1972), pp. 601-37.
10.   R. Redfield and M.B. Singer, 'The cultural role of cities , *Economic Development and Cultural Change*, 3 (1954), pp. 53-73; R. Redfield, *The Primitive World* (1953); *The Primitive World and its Transformations* (1953); *Peasant Society and Culture* (1956).
11.   David Harvey, *Social Justice and the City* (1973).
12.   See below, Chapter 3, and John Langton, 'Residential patterns in pre-industrial cities: some case studies from the seventeenth century', *Transactions, Institute of British Geographers*, 65 (1975), pp. 1-28.
13.   *The World of the Vikings*, National Maritime Museum, London (1973), p. 24.
14.   See A.T. Lucas, 'Plundering of Churches in Ireland', in E. Rynne (ed.), *North Munster Studies* (1967), pp. 172-229.
15.   P.H. Sawyer, 'The Vikings and the Irish Sea', in D. Moore (ed.), *The Irish Sea Province in Archaeology and History* (1970), p. 91.
16.   See D. Ellmers, 'The Ships of the Vikings', in *The World of the Vikings* (1973), pp. 13-14.
17.   Cited by Kathleen Hughes, *Early Christian Ireland: Introduction to the Sources* (1972), p. 151.
18.   D. O'Corrain, *Ireland before the Normans* (1972), p. 93.
19.   Ibid., p. 106.
20.   Lloyd Laing, *The Archaeology of Late Celtic Britain and Ireland* (1975), p. 229. See also R.H.M. Dolley, 'Viking coin hoards from Ireland and their relevance for Anglo-Saxon studies', in R.H.M. Dolley (ed.), *Anglo-Saxon Coins* (1961); *The Hiberno-Norse Coins in the British Museum* (1966); *Viking Coins of the Danelaw and of Dublin* (1965).
21.   *The World of the Vikings* (1973), p. 27.
22.   Details are given in: B. O'Riordain, 'Introduction' to C. Haliday, *The Scandinavian Kingdom of Dublin* (reprint, Shannon, 1969), pp. v-viii; *Current Archaeology*, 22 (1970), pp. 312-16; B. O'Riordain, 'Excavations at High Street and Winetavern Street, Dublin', *Medieval Archaeology*, XV (1971), pp. 73-86; *Viking and Medieval Dublin*, National Museum of Ireland (1973).
23.   G.H. Orpen, *Ireland Under the Normans* (1911), Vol. 1, pp. 247-71.
24.   Binchy, cited by Hughes, op. cit. (1972), p. 158.
25.   Ibid., p. 159.
26.   F. Byrne, *Irish Kings and High-Kings* (1973), p. 12.
27.   Ibid.

28. E.R.R. Green, 'Some agenda for Irish urban history', *Urban History Newsletter*, 9 (1967), p. 7.
29. C.T. Smith, *An Historical Geography of Western Europe* (1967), p. 86.
30. Byrne, op. cit., p. 12.
31. Binchy, op. cit.
32. G. Camblin, *The Town in Ulster* (1951), pp. 5-6.
33. Barry Raftery, 'Irish Hill-Forts', in Charles Thomas (ed.), *The Iron Age in the Irish Sea Province*, C.B.A. Research Reports No. 9 (1972), pp. 37-58.
34. Ibid., p. 45.
35. Byrne, op. cit., p. 7.
36. Ibid., p. 32.
37. Raftery, op. cit., p. 39.
38. Ibid., p. 43.
39. Ibid., p. 54.
40. Ibid., *passim*.
41. Ibid., p. 54.
42. John Morris, *The Age of Arthur* (1973), p. 373.
43. Ibid., p. 374.
44. E.R. Norman and J.K.S. St Joseph, *The Early Development of Irish Society* (1969), pp. 97-8.
45. T.W. Moody and F.X. Martin (eds.), *The Course of Irish History* (1967), p. 68.
46. Brian Graham, 'The Evolution of the Settlement Pattern of Anglo-Norman Eastmeath', in R.H. Buchanan, R.A. Butlin and D. McCourt (eds.), *Fields, Farms and Settlement in Europe* (1976), pp. 38-47; see below, Chapter 2.
47. Kathleen Hughes, op. cit., p. 178.
48. Camblin, op. cit., p. 7.
49. O'Corrain, op. cit., p. 88.
50. Bruce Proudfoot, 'Excavations at the Cathedral Hill, Downpatrick, Co. Down', *Ulster Journal of Archaeology*, 19 (1956), pp. 71-2.

2 THE TOWNS OF MEDIEVAL IRELAND

B.J. Graham

Introduction

At the beginning of May 1169, a small force of Anglo-Norman soldiers, under the command of Robert Fitz Stephen, landed at Bannow Bay, Co. Wexford, an event which initiated an attempted conquest of Ireland. Despite the subsequent failure of this venture, the Normans made a vitally important contribution to the development of an urban system in the island, for the invasion was followed in later years by an influx of settlers which led directly to a century of new-town building.

Little is known of the settlements associated with the pre-Norman indigenous culture but it is assumed that, at the time of the Norman invasion, the Irish lived in dispersed farmsteads (some of which were located in ring-forts[1]) and nucleated agricultural settlements of which the later clachans were probably descendants.[2] There were some semblance' to native urbanised settlements at some of the more important monasteries. In the Irish *Annals*, the destruction of towns, as distinct from churches, was often recorded at such sites. In 1135, for example, Ros-Commain (Roscommon) 'was plundered and burned, both houses and churches',[3] while in 976, 'the abbey and town' of Kells, Co. Meath, was plundered by the Danes.[4] These settlements were not urban in the same sense as the later Norman foundations with their legally granted charters and their organised urban institutions. Nevertheless, such centres did act as foci for nucleated settlements which were, perhaps, the homes of lay craftsmen and agricultural labourers employed by the monasteries.

Prior to the arrival of the Normans, however, several urban settlements had been established in Ireland by the Norse who had first appeared around the coasts in the ninth and tenth centuries. They carried out raids, particularly upon the rich monasteries of the Irish early Christian church but, due to their loose tribal organisation, the Irish were unable to offer any effective resistance; however, the Norse did not attempt to conquer Ireland. Rather, they established and settled in a number of walled coastal towns of which Dublin, Wexford, Waterford, Cork and Limerick were the most important. The Norse continued to hold these towns, which acted as trading stations, until the Norman invasion, and three of them — Wexford, Waterford and Dublin – provided the Normans with their first strongholds in Ireland.

Therefore, the growth of towns which took place throughout the greater part of Ireland during the early medieval period was almost entirely due to Norman influence. In this chapter, the historical evolution of this movement of new-town building is examined and the spatial distribution pattern and characteristics of the new towns themselves are discussed. Unavoidably, this discussion is very much of an exploratory nature and is restricted to the general rather than to the specific.

Research into the medieval settlement of Ireland has been very much neglected in the past and comparatively little is known of Irish medieval towns, despite the importance of the period to the genesis of the urban system within the island. Two major obstacles are apparent in discussing the towns of this period. The first is a question of semantics, namely, the definition of *town* and *urban* within the context of medieval Ireland. In view of a lack of data which would permit a functional classification of the Norman settlements of the island, it appears that the most satisfactory definition of *town* is a settlement which possessed borough status with a corporation and privileges conferred by a charter.

The grant of such a charter was normally a royal prerogative but, in medieval Ireland, the right to create a borough in this way was often exercised by sub-tenants of the Crown. For example, Walter de Lacy, Lord of Meath, granted charters to the boroughs of Kells and Trim between 1194 and 1199[5] and William Marshal granted a charter to the burgesses of Moone, Co. Kildare, *circa* 1223.[6] Some boroughs were also founded by churchmen; for example, Cloyne and Kilmaclennan, Co. Cork, were both granted charters by the Bishop of Cloyne in 1251,[7] whilst the borough of Rathcoole, Co. Dublin, was incorporated by the Archbishop of Dublin *circa* 1245.[8] It was not, in fact, until the fifteenth century that it became necessary to obtain royal authority in order to create a borough. The problem of definition is that many of the boroughs, thus created, do not appear to have possessed *urban* characteristics. The most common Norman settlement form in Ireland was the small agriculturally orientated manorial village, and on the basis of the extant evidence, it appears that many of the medieval boroughs were never more than manorial villages in morphology or function. However, they were granted the elements of an urban constitution which, Otway-Ruthven suggests, made it easier to attract settlers from Britain by offering the bait of burgess status.[9] This involved a considerable array of privileges, the most important of which included the grant of burgage holdings at an annual rent of one shilling a year, the right of burgesses to their own hundred court and a share in the common fields. This particular set of privileges was known as the *Law of Breteuil*, although several of the more important towns, including Dublin, were granted the same privileges as the port of Bristol, which included the rights to form merchant guilds and to have trade monopolies.[10] Glasscock uses the term 'rural-borough' to describe these pseudo-urban settlements but does not clarify the criteria which might be utilised to differentiate between rural-boroughs and boroughs which had true urban characteristics.[11] Within the specific context of this discussion, it is impossible, due to a lack of accurate data pertaining to functions and population, to formulate such a valid set of criteria in order to define this dichotomy. Further, it is felt that the term rural-borough itself is not particularly valid, because the central consideration in this case is to examine the movement of new-town building in medieval Ireland. The so-called rural-boroughs, whatever their eventual array of functions, must be considered as part of this movement and can be regarded as urban speculations which failed for various economic and historical reasons.

The second major problem in discussing the towns of medieval Ireland is the nature of the historical sources. Not only is there a general paucity of extant documentary sources which contain information that is relevant to urban settlement but there is also an areal imbalance in those sources which have survived. Some areas are particularly poorly documented in this respect, especially Meath and Louth, in which it is possible to do no more than identify the boroughs. Such deficiencies hinder comparisons between different areas and prevent a representative discussion of the relative importance of the medieval towns of the island.

The Historical Evolution of Towns in Medieval Ireland

The processes of foundation and subsequent growth of the medieval towns were inseparable concomitants of the political history of the Norman colony. It is clear that the majority of the urban foundations took place within the first century after the initial invasion of the island, as the Normans advanced rapidly from their initial strong points of Dublin, Wexford and Waterford. Settlement proper began after the Treaty of Windsor, signed in 1175 between Henry II, King of England, and Rory O'Connor, the last but nominal High King of Ireland. Under the terms of the treaty, Dublin, Meath,[12] Leinster[13] and Waterford as far west as Dungarvan were reserved to the Normans. These were the first areas to be colonised but the Norman advance rapidly moved beyond them. In 1177, Ulster was invaded by John de Courcy and in the 1180s the settlement of east Cork began. By 1190, the coast from Drogheda to Cork was in Norman hands and in Leinster this occupation extended far inland. By 1200, the occupation of Limerick and Tipperary was well on the way to consolidation, the Norse (or Ostman) town of Limerick being occupied in 1196 (it was briefly held by Raymond le Gros in 1176 but was soon abandoned). After 1200, the territorial expansion slowed as the invaders began to move into areas such as west Ulster and Cavan, which they were never to hold successfully. The first tentative movements across the Shannon began and Kerry was also occupied, whilst later, *circa* 1220, there was a more important movement into Clare. The last area to be colonised by the Normans was Connaught, the conquest of which was complete in 1235; with this final step the Norman territorial expansion in Ireland can be said to have reached its peak.[14]

Once the Normans had achieved a degree of military control over an area, the mechanics of settlement evolution began. The customary preliminary stage was the grant of large areas of land by the Crown to principal tenants. Leinster, for example, was granted to the Earl of Pembroke (better known as Strongbow) by Henry II in 1171 whilst, in the following year, the King granted Meath to Hugh de Lacy. Once a great fief such as Meath had been granted to the principal tenant of the Crown, its sub-infeudation took place; that is, various areas within it were granted to smaller sub-tenants.[15] In addition, the principal tenants retained large areas of these lordships for themselves. As the Normans advanced across Ireland, similar processes took place elsewhere, although there were areal variations. North Munster (Limerick and Tipperary), for example, was not initially granted in one vast fief to a single grantee; rather, it was parcelled out directly by King John into a number of smaller grants.[16] The secondary land grants of the sub-infeudations of the various lordships were further subdivided into manors, the manor being the basic land division of Norman Ireland. The delineation of the varying land units was the first stage in the colonisation and settlement of the conquered lands, because it was within this framework that the establishment of settlements, some of which eventually achieved borough status, occurred. The significance of this hierarchical system of land grants was that it pre-dated the foundation of settlements and, hence, exercised an extremely powerful control over settlement location and the subsequent development of the settlement pattern.

In the process of settlement evolution, the preliminary land alloca-
tions were followed by a second stage which involved the construction
of military strongholds; in the early period of the conquest, at least,
these were generally motte-and-bailey castles,[17] which were erected by
the grantees in order to consolidate control over their lands. This
second stage of military consolidation initially took place in the
seigniorial manors, retained by the principal tenants, and in the grants
of the primary sub-infeudations before these were divided into manors.
Therefore, there were time differentials within each area between the
establishment of settlements associated with the primary and secondary
land grants.

Once a degree of military control, and therefore security, had been
established, settlers began arriving and primeval settlements, many of
which were never to become more than manorial villages, began to
grow up around the motte castles and manorial churches. The villages
were typically the secondary settlements, associated with the minor
levels in the land division hierarchy. The majority of Norman settlements in Ireland did not pass beyond this stage. The penultimate stage
in this evolutionary process was the royal grant to a sub-tenant of the
right to hold a weekly market and yearly fair at his settlement, thereby
investing it with an important economic function. There are numerous
examples of such grants in the documents of the period; for example in
1226, Andrew Blundes was granted a weekly market and yearly fair at
his manor of Kinsale, Co. Cork,[18] while in 1234, Maurice Fitz Gerald
was granted a similar charter at his manor of Yohyll (Youghal), Co.
Cork.[19]

The final stage was the grant of a charter which conferred borough
status, although, as noted above, this cannot be taken to indicate that
the settlement was necessarily *urban* in its functions or morphology.
Most of the settlements which obtained such charters were located at
the sites of the initial military strongholds, associated with the seigniorial manors and the land grants of primary sub-infeudations. Settlements at these sites possessed inherent advantages, both of time and of
location, in their development compared with the secondary settlements of the manorial level of land subdivision. The dates of the grants
of charters can be used as an index of the foundation of medieval urban
settlements in Ireland; unfortunately in some cases the earliest extant
charters are not, in fact, the originals. The Anglo-Norman municipal
system in the island began with Henry II's charter to Dublin, granted at
some time between November 1171 and March 1172.[20] Before the end
of the twelfth century several other charters had been attested; for

example, Drogheda,[21] Kells[22] and Trim,[23] all in the Liberty of Meath, were incorporated between 1194 and 1199 as was Swords, Co. Dublin,[24] whilst Cork received its first charter between 1189 and 1199.[25] After 1210, a number of settlements in Leinster were incorporated including Kilkenny *circa* 1211,[26] Kells, Co. Kilkenny, between 1211 and 1216,[27] Carlow in 1223[28] (although it is probable that there were burgesses here before the end of the twelfth century and, therefore, this may not be the original charter[29]) and Inistiog, Co. Kilkenny, in 1228.[30] In all, there are extant records of about thirty such charters although it should be noted that there are no surviving records of the charters which were granted to the majority of boroughs.

However, *circa* 1220, it is clear that primitive urban settlements were well established in at least those parts of Ireland which were subinfeudated soon after the initial invasion. In some cases such as Meath, there was only a short time interval between the land subdivisions and the grants of borough charters; obviously it was in the interests of the grantees to obtain borough status for their settlements as rapidly as possible. As the Normans advanced across Ireland, the same process continued although, unfortunately, there are no extant charters to boroughs such as Tralee, Bunratty and Sligo which would aid the dating of the foundation of urban settlements at the extremities of Norman influence. The indissoluble link between the land-holding system and the foundation of urban settlements in Ireland is central to an understanding of the historical settlement geography of the period and the influence of this pre-existing framework must always be borne in mind when discussing the distribution and location of the medieval towns of the island.

Distribution and Location

Utilising the evidence of charters and the occurrence of burgesses in settlement populations, 172 boroughs have been recorded (Appendix 1); it is certain that this inventory is not exhaustive because there were undoubtedly further boroughs of which there are no extant records. In addition, it is probable that a further 52 settlements, which received grants of weekly markets, can be added to this list because such a grant is strong, although not definitive, evidence that the settlement possessed borough status.

The inexact nature of the evidence and, in particular, the biases caused by the areal inequality of the extant sources precludes a statistical analysis of the medieval distribution of boroughs. However, density ratios of boroughs and settlements which had received grants of weekly markets were calculated (the number of square miles to each settlement, by counties); it should be noted that these ratios are no more than a general guide because of unreliable data. Nevertheless, they do exhibit distinct trends, particularly with respect to the comparative intensity of the distribution of boroughs in the various areas colonised by the Normans. Maximum borough densities occurred in the three eastern counties of Louth, Kildare and Dublin which, together with Meath, formed the most stable and intensively settled area of the colony. This high-density area was followed by a zone of intermediate density, comprising the counties of Kilkenny, Meath, Wexford, Tipperary, Cork, Carlow and Limerick, all of which were settled thoroughly and early in the Norman advance through Ireland. Finally, there was a low-density group, ranging from Westmeath and the mountainous eastern county of Wicklow, much of which remained in Irish hands throughout the medieval period despite its proximity to Dublin, to Kerry in the far south-west. Most of these counties were on the fringes of Norman expansion, even in the mid-thirteenth century when the colony had reached its maximum territorial extent. Therefore, in general, the density of boroughs attained its maximum in eastern and south-eastern Ireland and declined in all directions to the west and north as the intensity of Norman settlement became less and less in the face of the military difficulties of holding these fringe areas against the Irish. Hence, considerable areas of the island, particularly in the central lowlands and in the north-west and west, did not participate in the characteristic medieval development of urbanisation. The impact of the new-town movement was restricted to the English areas and reached its maximum intensity in the most Anglicised area around Dublin.

Due to the operation of various macro- and micro-scale variables, the distribution map of medieval boroughs (Figure 3) displays considerable variations, even within those areas which were intensively settled by the invaders. For example, their boroughs were noticeably absent from upland areas (the upper limit of Norman settlement in Ireland was around 500 ft. or 180m.[31]) and from the low-lying Central Plain. Within areas which were environmentally favourable, several micro-scale variables were of considerable significance in their influence upon the detailed siting of boroughs. The overriding synthesising factor was the association of boroughs with locations which possessed strategic value, the result of the link between the evolution of the settlement pattern and the existence of the pre-existing, hierarchical framework of land units. Almost invariably the military strong point, the first stage of actual settlement in any particular land unit irrespective of its level

Table 1: Density Ratios, by County, of Boroughs and Settlements with Weekly Markets

County	Area (sq. miles)	Number of boroughs	Number of settlements with weekly markets	Density Ratio	Rank
Louth	316	10	2	26 : 1	1
Kildare	654	22	1	28 : 1	2
Dublin	375	11	0	34 : 1	3
Kilkenny	792	14	3	46 : 1	4
Meath	903	15	4	47 : 1	5
Wexford	896	13	2	59 : 1	6
Tipperary	1639	19	3	74 : 1	7
Cork	2873	10	28	76 : 1	8
Carlow	346	4	0	86 : 1	9
Limerick	1033	12	0	86 : 1	9
Leix	289	3	0	96 : 1	11
Westmeath	678	3	4	97 : 1	12
Wicklow	781	7	0	111 : 1	13
Waterford	713	4	1	143 : 1	14
Antrim	1106	6	0	184 : 1	15
Galway	1616	8	0	202 : 1	16
Roscommon	912	4	0	228 : 1	17
Down	959	3	1	240 : 1	18
Clare	1205	1	2	402 : 1	19
Longford	403	0	1	403 : 1	20
Sligo	706	1	0	706 : 1	21
Kerry	1815	2	0	907 : 1	22

in the hierarchy, was sited at a location of strategic significance. Hence, the settlements which post-dated this initial stage were also sited at essentially strategic locations because economic considerations only assumed importance after the establishment of settlement and the organisation of agriculture in the colonised lands. Fortunately for the future welfare of many of the medieval boroughs, sites of strategic importance often corresponded with sites which were of economic value.

Within the confines of this overriding strategic control, a detailed statistical analysis of the medieval settlement pattern of Meath revealed several variables which were shown to have exerted significant influences upon the location of Norman settlements, namely the distributions of river-crossings, navigable rivers and pre-Norman monastic sites.[32] A distribution map of medieval settlements in the area, both boroughs (of which there were fifteen including rural-borough) and manorial villages, was compiled and was overlain by a fine mesh of quadrats which were used as data collection units, not only for the three variables noted above but also for others peculiar to Meath, the most important of which was the existence of a frontier zone. These units were of a sufficiently small size to permit two assumptions, first that the variables within them were homogeneous and second, that if a settlement occurred within a quadrat, the values of the variables for the quadrat as a whole were those which obtained at the specific point in space at which the settlement was located. The advantage of this method over collecting the environmental data relating to the settlements at the actual locations was that points at which settlements were not sited were also included in the analysis. As settlement locations reflect the interaction of particular variables at particular points in space, it was only logical to examine those points at which settlements did not occur in order to determine whether or not differing combinations of the same variables repelled settlements. As the use of this quadrat data collection method reduced all variables to a discrete form, chi-square tests were utilised to test the null hypotheses that there was no association between the distributions of settlements and river-crossings, navigable rivers and pre-Norman monastic sites (Table 2); the chi-square 2 x 2 contingency test was used.

These same variables were also apparently significant in accounting for the development of boroughs at particular locations elsewhere in Norman Ireland. In a heavily wooded landscape such as Ireland at the time of the invasion, a navigable river is often the most advantageous means of transport. By controlling such rivers and also the bridging points and fords where land routes crossed them, the Normans effectively controlled movement. Consequently, in Meath, as shown above, the distribution of settlements and particularly of boroughs displayed a high degree of positive correlation, both with the distribution of river-crossing points, and with the Boyne, which was navigable from the sea at Drogheda as far inland as Trim.[33] Many of the other major rivers of Ireland were also navigable in the medieval period, although most are no longer so. The Barrow, for example, was used by small boats from the sea at New Ross as far inland as Athy,[34] whilst the Suir was navigable at least as far inland as Clonmel;[35] other rivers used for transport included the Liffey,[36] the Blackwater[37] and the Slaney, which was navigable as far inland as Enniscorthy.

Table 2: Tests of Association between the Distribution of Norman Settlements in Meath and the Distributions of River-crossings, Navigable Rivers and Pre-Norman Monastic Sites

Variable	Quadrats with occurences of settlements and variables	Quadrats with occurrence of variable only	Quadrats with occurrence of settlement only	Quadrats without occurrences of settlements or variables	Result
River-crossings	31	25	68	285	34.32
Navigable rivers	16	16	83	294	12.60
Pre-Norman monastic sites	22	4	77	306	55.23

All results were significant at the .001 level.

The positive correlation between the distribution of pre-Norman monastic sites and boroughs in Meath was presumably due to the fact that when the Normans first colonised the area they were attracted to these sites as the monasteries formed the only nucleated settlements in a predominantly rural landscape and it was the settlements associated with the first stages of colonisation which most often became boroughs. In addition, the monasteries were often sited at riverine locations which would have been attractive to the Normans in any case.

Empirical analysis of the 163 borough sites which have been identified (nine sites remain unidentified because of desertions and place-name

vagaries) indicated that the micro-scale variables found to be of importance in Meath can also be utilised to partially explain the distribution
of Norman boroughs elsewhere in Ireland. Seventy-seven boroughs
(47.2 per cent of the total) were sited, either at coastal locations or on
the banks of navigable rivers; a further 24 (14.7 per cent) were sited on
non-navigable rivers. In total, 55 boroughs (33.7 per cent) were sited at
riverine locations, indicating the influence of the distributions of both
navigable waterways and river-crossing points upon the Norman
decision-making process. (It is impossible to be precise about the
influence of river-crossing points because of changes in the physical
environment since the medieval period.)

In addition, many of the medieval settlements which became important boroughs were located at the sites of pre-Norman monasteries. The
town of Kilkenny, for example, grew up on the site of the early church
and monastery of St Canice,[38] while the borough of Roscrea, Co.
Tipperary, was located at the site of the early monastery of St Cronan.[39]
Presumably, given the attractions of the principal river valleys to the
invaders, bridging points, fords and the pre-existing monastic nuclea-
tions determined exact sites. However, almost 40 per cent of the
boroughs were not related to these locational factors, which indicates
the importance of the pre-existing framework of land units in controlling settlement location. Settlements had to be sited within the confines of the land grants, irrespective of the non-occurrence of these
desirable locational attributes. Hence, these micro-scale variables can
only account for the locations of some boroughs; there was, necessarily,
a random set of location factors, related to the land-holding system.

Urban Functions

The boroughs of medieval Ireland possessed three basic groups of
functions which were characteristically urban, namely, general economic functions, specialised economic functions and military functions.
The level at which a particular borough practised these functions was a
reflection of the adaptability of its basic strategic location to the economic network which followed the establishment of organised systems
of agriculture and trade.

The general economic functions performed by all boroughs irrespective of size were principally associated with agriculture for, within
Ireland, the Norman settlers developed a semi-commercial system of
agriculture, exporting animal products and even foodstuffs to England.
The inland boroughs acted as the centres of trade and exchange and as
the collecting points for agricultural produce, which was then moved to

the ports of the south and east coast for shipment to England. The typical goods which were exchanged in the borough markets were corn, cattle and hides, fish, cloth, metals and foodstuffs.[40] Many of these markets could only have operated at the local scale but those boroughs which were sited on routeways, particularly the navigable rivers, acted as regional collecting centres through which agricultural products for export were shipped to the coast and imported English manufactured goods were distributed to the smaller local markets. Mills were found in most boroughs, processing local agricultural produce for local consumption, but in some of the larger boroughs agricultural products were processed for export.

The most important boroughs, which were, in general, the ports, possessed specialised economic functions which contributed, in conjunction with their superior locational attributes, to their pre-eminence in the urban system. As Ireland was a colony to be settled and exploited, the ports provided the links, both with England and with Europe, through which this could be achieved; the maximum array of economic functions could then be developed. The most extensive section of Ireland's trade was that carried on by the southern ports of New Ross, Waterford, Youghal and Cork with England and, in particular, with the port of Bristol. The principal cargoes which they exported were of fish, hides and skins, whilst in the reverse direction, Bristol exported cloth, salt, wine and some food to Ireland.[41] Further north, Dublin and Drogheda exported skins, hides, fish and linen to Chester and Liverpool.[42] The ports of Ulster, the most important of which was Carrickfergus,[43] carried on their trade with Scotland and the north of England, whilst, in the west, Galway imported wine directly from Europe, particularly from Bordeaux,[44] although this trade was later extended to include Spain and Portugal.[45]

A detailed study of the medieval ports of Ireland is of some significance because it provides an insight into the relative importance of the most important boroughs of the Norman colony. There are few extant records of actual goods and tonnages carried but the Crown levied customs on goods shipped through the various ports. The extan returns which are contained in the Pipe Rolls cover the period 1276-1333, and these can be used as an index of the relative importance of each port (Table 3).[46]

It is apparent that the medieval ports fell into three distinct groups. The first comprised New Ross and Waterford, which was by far the most important, accounting for marginally over 50 per cent of total Irish trade (if it is assumed that the customs returns are an accurate

Figure 3: The Distribution of Medieval Boroughs in Ireland, c. 1300

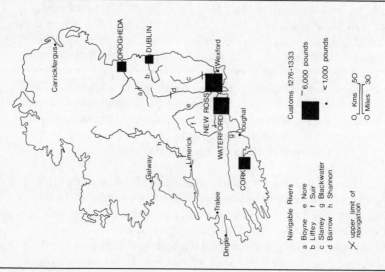

Burgess household populations

□ over 1000
□ 500-999
● below 500
● unknown

0 kms 40
0 mls 25

Figure 4: Medieval Irish Ports

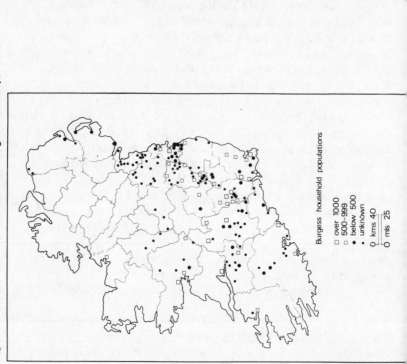

Carrickfergus

DROGHEDA
DUBLIN

a
b
c
Wexford
d
e
NEW ROSS
f
WATERFORD
g
Youghal

Limerick
Galway
h
CORK

Tralee

Dingle

Navigable Rivers

a Boyne   e Nore
b Liffey   f Suir
c Slaney g Blackwater
d Barrow h Shannon

✕ upper limit of
   navigation

Customs 1276-1333

■ 6,000 pounds
● <1,000 pounds

0 Kms 50
0 Miles 30

Table 3: Customs Returns of Irish Ports, 1276-1333

Port	Total Customs paid by each port between 1276 and 1333 (to nearest pound)	Percentage of total customs paid	Rank
New Ross	5,928	26.08	1
Waterford	5,514	24.31	2
Cork	3,909	17.24	3
Drogheda	3,115	13.73	4
Dublin	2,512	11.10	5
Youghal	691	3.05	6
Ulster Ports	408	1.80	7
Galway	341	1.50	8
Limerick	142	0.63	9
Kerry Ports[47]	88	0.39	10
Wexford	40	0.17	11

index of this trade). Second, there was a group comprising Cork, Drogheda and Dublin which was of intermediate importance and accounted for a further 42.07 per cent of the total trade. Finally, the remaining four ports, Youghal, Galway, Limerick and Wexford, plus the ports of Ulster and Kerry, accounted for only 7.54 per cent of total trade (Figure 4).

Each of the five major ports, Drogheda, Dublin, New Ross, Waterford and Cork, served a distinct hinterland to which each was linked by a navigable river. Together, these hinterlands comprised the most densely settled and prosperous areas of the Norman colony. Drogheda, at the mouth of the Boyne, served Meath and Louth while Dublin, at the mouth of the Liffey, presumably served north Leinster. New Ross and Waterford, the former sited at the confluence of the Nore and the Barrow and the latter at the mouth of the Suir, served most of the interior of south-east Ireland and finally Cork, at the head of the Lee Estuary, was the port for much of the south-west. The remainder, with the exceptions of Youghal, which served a small area along the south coast, and Wexford, were located in areas of Ireland in which Norman colonisation never achieved the same intensity as in the east and south-east. The position of Wexford as the least important port at which customs were collected is puzzling because the town is generally regarded as having been one of the most important medieval boroughs. The explanation appears to lie in its small hinterland which was restricted to the area immediately around the town for, to the north, the Wicklow Mountains remained in Irish hands, while to the west, Waterford and New Ross had developed at more favourable locations to serve the interior of Leinster. These specialised functions provided the five major ports with economic advantages which made them more important than *any* of the inland boroughs.

It has already been shown that as the medieval settlement pattern evolved, boroughs tended to develop at locations which had been initially selected because of their strategic value; many of the towns retained the military importance of their sites throughout the history of the colony. In areas where the Norman hold was not secure, settlement was virtually restricted to the fortified towns and control over the surrounding countryside was very much more transitory. Even in the more secure areas, the role of the larger boroughs as citadels was a continued necessity because the history of medieval Ireland was characterised by constant warfare between the Irish and the settlers and also by equally constant internecine warfare within both groups. Murage charters, which were granted by the Crown, provide evidence of the construction of town defences. Under the terms of these charters, citizens were empowered to levy customs on goods passing through their towns in order to construct or repair defences. Over thirty such charters are extant but they do not generally detail the nature of the defences nor, of course, does the grant of a murage charter provide historical evidence of the actual construction of defences. However, such was the insecurity of the Norman position in Ireland (an insecurity which markedly increased in the fourteenth and fifteenth centuries) that most of the boroughs except, perhaps, for the very smallest, probably had some form of defence. Castledermot, Co. Kildare, for example, which received a grant of murage in 1295,[48] had a population of less than 500 at that date.[49] In these small boroughs, it is likely that the defences were composed of an earthen enclosing bank, topped with wooden palisades.[50] In a grant of murage to Kilmallock, Co. Limerick, in 1374, it is mentioned that the former wall structures were destroyed by fire and were, therefore, probably of this type.[51]

However, the larger boroughs had much more substantial defences of stone walls and protected gates. For example, the twin towns of Drogheda, one on either bank of the Boyne, were protected by a substantial stone wall in which there was a total of six gates; other important towns such as Dublin, Waterford, New Ross, Cork and Limerick were all protected in this fashion.

Internal Organisation

We lack any contemporary documentary accounts of the internal
organisation of the medieval towns of Ireland, particularly with regard
to their physical plans and to population size and structure and, in
addition, with the notable exception of the important excavations at
High Street and Winetavern Street in Dublin, there has been virtually
no archaeological investigation of the structure of the medieval
boroughs. At the peak of their medieval expansion, the areas within
the walls of the larger boroughs such as Dublin and Drogheda must
have been densely inhabited. However, relatively little is known about
these urban populations and there appears to have been considerable
variation from borough to borough in their social compositions. For
example, at New Ross, the burgesses lived both within and without the
walls, which may reflect the prosperity of the medieval town as it
suggests that population growth had outstripped the area of the walled
town.[52] At Cork, however, the privileges under the charter were clearly
granted only to those who lived within the walls.[53] It appears that most
of the burgesses were immigrants and although the Irish certainly lived
in towns, they appear, at least in the early years of the colony to have
possessed limited social standing. However, at Kilkenny there were two
distinct burgess settlements; in 1307, the burgesses of the town paid
£11.15s. 4d. in rent but, in addition, those of St John's Street paid
£4.13s. 11d.[54] It is possible that the latter set of burgesses were Irish
because Edward IV later granted the right of choosing their own
portreeve to Irishtown in Kilkenny.[55] There are several other examples
of Irish burgesses and it appears in the later years of the colony that the
proportion of Irish burgesses in the boroughs increased.[56] The descendants of the Norse (known as Ostmen) lived in separate settlements
outside the port towns; for example, the town of the Ostmen at
Waterford is referred to in extant documents as a suburb.[57]

Again, the analysis of urban population size is hindered both by
inadequate and also inexact data. For example, there is not a solitary
borough for which the exact medieval population size is known. In
general, the only extant data relates to the burgess populations and
even these must be computed from details of burgage rents; if this is
known, the number of burgesses in a settlement can be readily calculated because each generally paid one shilling per annum for his
burgage plot.[58] For example, in 1307 when the burgage rent of Carlow
was £8.0s.16½d. there should have been 161 burgesses living in the

town; in fact there were 8 score or 160.[59] Again, in 1308, the burgage
rent of Carrick-on-Slaney, Co. Wexford, was 111s.9d. (approximately
111 burgesses) and there were actually 110 burgages.[60] A particular
problem is that details of rent of this type only relate to the number of
actual burgesses and not to the burgesses plus their households. Therefore, in order to arrive at a crude estimate of total population, an
assumed average family size of 5 is used below.[61]

In the examples above and in the majority of such cases, the number
of burgesses can be calculated simply and accurately from details of
burgage rent. However, there are certain cases where the burgage rent
appears to be misleading and must have included payment, for example,
for land in addition to that held in the burgage plots. For instance, the
burgesses of Dunfert, Co. Kildare, rendered £23.9s.4½d. in 1307;[62]
theoretically, the settlement had 409 burgesses, which is most unlikely
as there is no other evidence to support the contention that this settlement was anything other than a small rural-borough. Again, the
burgesses of Dungarvan, Co. Waterford, paid £13.17s.4d. in 1282[63] and
a similar amount in 1299.[64] rents which represent a theoretical burgess
household population of about 1,885. Again, there is no other evidence
to support the contention that Dungarvan was one of the three or four
most important boroughs in medieval Ireland.

In addition to these problems, which are related to the ambiguous
nature of the data, further difficulties arise because of areal disparities
in extant details of burgage rent. There are relatively good data for
some areas, and in particular for Limerick, Tipperary, Carlow, Wexford
and Kilkenny[65] while, at the same time, there are virtually no extant
details of burgess rents for other areas, notably Cork, Meath and Louth.
Hence, comparisons in the populations of medieval towns between the
various regions of Norman Ireland are difficult and, in view of the
inexact evidence relating to functions, this causes particular problems in
attempting to estimate the relative importance of the towns of the
medieval colony.

A further problem is that the burgesses were not the only inhabitants
of the boroughs. The population of Forth, Co. Carlow, for example,
comprised 29 cottagers (farm labourers) in addition to its 75 burgesses;[66] again, the borough of Lusk, Co. Dublin contained 46 cottagers
in addition to 36 burgages[67] while the population of Swords, Co.
Dublin, was composed of 122 burgesses, 16 free cottagers and 28
gavellors (tenants-at-will).[68] Presumably, many of the other boroughs
had similar mixtures of social classes within their populations but,
unfortunately, not only are extant data relating to these other classes

often unavailable, but their proportions in the total populations varied from borough to borough so that it is impossible to use a constant to arrive at a more accurate estimation of the borough populations. At Ardmayle, Co. Tipperary, for example, almost the entire recorded population of the borough were burgesses which may explain the somewhat high rent of £17.3s. paid in 1305 (equivalent to a burgess household population of about 1,715).[69] Conversely, at Mayglass, Co. Wexford, there were only 10 burgesses and the bulk of the population was composed of cottagers, farmers and betaghs (serfs).[70]

One attempt has been made to estimate the populations of medieval Irish towns and to rank them but this suffered not only from its attempt to prove a pre-existing hypothesis which the extant data do not support, but also from the inexact nature of these data. These may only be utilised to make general statements about comparative populations and cannot, under any circumstances, be used to produce accurate rankings of medieval boroughs.[71] Dublin, which was the seat of government of the colony, was presumably the foremost borough, both in terms of area and of population size. Russell notes that the average medieval borough contained about 100–120 persons to the hectare, although in towns of less than 3,000 density tended to be lower than 100 to the hectare.[72] He estimates that the medieval city of Dublin had an area of about 112 hectares, and allowing for areas of public buildings, this means that the population was around 10,000. This hypothetical figure would appear to be somewhat exaggerated as the area of the walled town was only 18 hectares,[73] although some of the population must have lived outside the defences. There is no accurate evidence of population size for several other important medieval towns including Limerick, Cork, Drogheda and Waterford, although in view of the evidence from other towns, it seems probable that all four had burgess household populations of between 1,000 and 2,000.

After Dublin, despite the uncertainty of the evidence, it can be stated that New Ross was the second-largest medieval town in terms of population size. In 1307, the burgesses of the town paid £25.6s.8d. for their burgages, which, within the confines of the assumptions noted above, is equivalent to a burgess household population of about 2,530.[74] Almost certainly the urban population was larger than this when other social groups were included. The burgess household population of Wexford appears to have reached a maximum of 1,800 at some time in the mid-thirteenth century. In 1307, there were 365½ burgages in the town, but, of these, 127 were waste;[75] the town must have undergone a rapid decline in the late thirteenth century because there were already 128½ waste burgages by 1298[76] and, by 1326, this figure had risen to 221½.[77] In this context, the customs returns for the period, 1276-1335, also indicated that Wexford was of minor importance and it appears that the Norman landlords may have been over-ambitious in their development of the town in view of its rather poor location. Kilkenny seems to have been the largest of the inland towns (if the figure for Ardmayle is put aside as being suspect), its total burgage rent of £16.9s.3d. in 1307 indicating a burgess household population of between 1,600 and 1,700.[78] Youghal paid a burgage rent of £12 in 1288, indicating a burgess household population of around 1,200;[79] Russell regards this as rather too high but it should be noted that the medieval town was the sixth port of the colony. Other boroughs which apparently had burgess household populations of more than 1,000 included Bunratty,[80] Co. Clare, Nenagh[81] and Thurles,[82] Co. Tipperary, and Galway.

In all, there are extant population data for 82 medieval boroughs; approximately 15 had burgess household populations of more than 1,000, 25 to 30 of between 500 and 1,000 and the remaining 35 to 40 of less than 500. Some general areal trends can be discerned from these figures (Table 4); the counties included are those which contained three or more boroughs with extant details of burgess population. Only boroughs which had burgess household populations of less than 1,000 are included. The figures are predictable in view of the historical background to the Norman colonisation of Ireland, although it must be noted that the three intensively colonised counties of Meath, Louth and Cork are excluded because of lack of evidence. The general conclusion which can be drawn from the figures is that there was a gradual decrease in intensity of borough settlement to the south-west and west. In terms of the introduction of urban settlements to Ireland, this can be interpreted as indicating that the speculative, medieval town foundations were most successful in the eastern and south-eastern counties, moderately successful in north Munster (Tipperary and Limerick). However, there are two striking anomalies to this general pattern which must be explained, the first being the relatively large populations of the towns of Connaught and the second the very small average size of the boroughs of Co. Dublin. There were only four boroughs with extant details of burgess household populations of less than 1,000 in Connaught which reflects the low intensity of Norman settlement in that area.[83] So precarious was the Norman hold that the settlers were concentrated in the small fortified boroughs and were not spread out in manorial villages as in the more secure areas of eastern Ireland. The very small size of the average burgess household population in Co. Dublin must reflect not only the overwhelming influence of the city of Dublin in the economic and population structure of the area, but also the vulnerability of the small boroughs of the southern area of the county to attacks by the Irish of the Wicklows.

Table 4: Average Size of Burgess Household Population for Boroughs of less than 1,000 Inhabitants

County	Number of settlements with extant details of burgess population	Average size of burgess household population
Kildare	7	733
Connaught (Galway & Sligo)	4	637
Wexford	10	565
Carlow	3	562
Kilkenny	7	435
Tipperary	6	392
Limerick	6	378
Dublin	8	212

Conclusions

Despite the limitations imposed upon the discussion of the urban characteristics of the boroughs of medieval Ireland by the nature of the extant evidence, it is possible, in general terms, to utilise these characteristics to examine the factors which contributed to the relative importance of the medieval boroughs to each other at the period of maximum expansion of the Norman colony in Ireland (*circa* 1250-1300). It is suggested that four factors controlled the relative status of a medieval Irish borough:

(a) its relationship with the historical process, particularly with the hierarchical nature of the land-holding system;
(b) the locational advantages of its site;
(c) its functions;

(d)   the size of its population.

The latter two factors can be regarded as the direct consequences of the operation of the former two factors.

As a general hypothesis, it can be stated that the relationship between the foundation of a settlement and the historical process was a primary determinant of its future status. When an economic system developed in medieval Ireland, the primary settlements sited at the initial strategic locations in the seigniorial manors and principal land grants of the various sub-infeudations possessed inherent locational advantages which often consolidated their primary military significance with a later economic importance. This can be illustrated by the example of the fief of Leinster, in which Strongbow retained the five seigniorial manors of Wexford, Ross, Kildare, Carlow and Dunamase in which he established primary settlements.[84] With the exception of the last-named, these became important boroughs, particularly the two ports of Ross and Wexford while the inland towns of Kildare and Carlow, although they did not possess the inherent locational advantages of the two coastal towns, were amongst the largest inland boroughs in medieval Ireland.[85] Strongbow granted considerable areas of land in the sub-infeudation of Leinster and, again in general, it can be stated that at this major level in the land-unit hierarchy there were related borough settlements which, in Leinster and elsewhere, were generally of less importance than the boroughs which had grown up at seigniorial manors. There are numerous examples of these boroughs (the phrase *caput baroniae* is sometimes used to describe such a settlement) in Leinster including Moone and Leixlip, both in Co. Kildare and Forth, Co. Carlow (Moone had a burgess household population of around 800 in 1305,[86] Leixlip of approximately 865 in 1331[87] and Forth of around 400 in 1307[88]). These major land units were further subdivided into manors and at this level in the land-holding system the majority of settlements remained manorial villages. However, several were incorporated as boroughs and these are probably the settlements which can best be regarded as rural-boroughs for they could only have been differentiated from manorial villages by their borough status and most were eventually destined to fail. Examples of this type of borough in Leinster included Cloncurry, Oughterard and Kilkea, all in Co. Kildare (Cloncurry had a burgess household population of approximately 560 in 1304,[89] Kilkea of as little as 135 in 1284;[90] that of Oughterard is not known). Therefore, it is suggested that the primary determinant of the relative importance of the boroughs of medieval Ireland was the successive subdivision of land. A further determinant, directly associated with this, was the decreasing range of preferences which could be exercised in settlement location. In the land units associated with the primary sub-infeudations of the various areas of Norman Ireland, relatively large areas of land were involved and, therefore, settlements were sited at the most advantageous locations within these areas; when these large areas were further subdivided into manors, the range of locational preferences were severely restricted. If, for example, a sub-tenant was granted an inland manor at some distance from a navigable river, the settlement which was established obviously did not benefit in its future growth from the presence of these desirable locational criteria. Therefore, even if the settlement eventually achieved borough status, its locational relationship with the pre-existing land-holding system militated against it attaining any real size or importance.

Hence it can be argued that the functions which developed within a particular borough and the population which it attracted were directly related to the interrelationship between location and the historical process. This relationship becomes clear if the burgess household populations are used as a general index of the importance of the medieval boroughs. Out of 15 or so boroughs with known burgess household populations in excess of 1,000, 13 were sited either at coastal locations or on navigable rivers and, in general, these were primary settlements, associated with major units in the land-holding system. Approximately 25 to 30 boroughs had known burgess household populations of between 500 and 1,000 and only about 50 per cent of these were sited at coastal locations or on navigable rivers. Of the 35 to 40 boroughs with known burgess household populations of less than 500, only 40 per cent were sited at these desirable locations. Therefore, as burgess household population size decreased, there was also a decrease in the correlation of the boroughs with the locational criteria which were of most importance to the Normans, illustrating the importance of the relationship between the historical process and location to the relative status within Norman Ireland of any particular medieval borough.

These factors contributed to the relative importance of boroughs within the movement of new-town foundation and building which the Normans brought to Ireland. How successful was this movement? After the peak of Norman territorial expansion and borough development, *circa* 1250, the situation remained fairly static, the Normans controlling about two-thirds of the island. There was, however, an Irish resurgence in the latter half of the thirteenth century and the situation was made worse by quarrels amongst the Anglo-Irish themselves; in addition, the

colony was in severe financial straits.[91] The earliest indications of
decline in some of the new boroughs were in the south-east in Wexford.
Although such declines may not have been solely restricted to this
region, we do not have comparable evidence from other areas. The
town of Wexford itself was already in decline before the end of the
thirteenth century, as was Ferns in which there were 49½ waste
burgages out of a total of 160 in 1298.[92] By 1307, the burgesses of
Rosbergen (on the western bank of the Barrow opposite New Ross)
were paying only 60s. burgage rent 'because of the war', compared
with a peace-time rent of £8.4s.11½d.[93]

In 1315, Edward Bruce invaded Ireland and during the three years
before his defeat in 1318 many of the boroughs suffered looting and
burning. After this event, the ever-increasing lawlessness was indicative
both of the decline of the colony as a whole and of the boroughs. By
1326, Ferns and Carrick-on-Slaney, Co. Wexford, were totally wasted
because of attacks by the Irish,[94] while several of the small boroughs
around Dublin were in a similar position. For example, at Dalkey, no
burgage rent could be levied in 1326 because of 'war' (presumably with
the Irish of the Wicklows) and the small boroughs of Burgage and
Kilmacberne in Co. Wicklow were almost destroyed at the same time.[95]
By 1333, most of the boroughs of Ulster, such as the Ford (Belfast)
and Greencastle, were burnt and destroyed and the burgesses of
Carrickfergus, the most important town of Ulster, were paying only
£2.16s.8d. (equivalent to 56 burgesses).[96]

Many of the boroughs which were in difficulties were small and on
the fringes of the area of Norman control but the evidence of the
customs returns, which display a steady decline from 1276 to 1333,
indicate that the larger boroughs were also affected. For example, in
1276-7, £743 was collected at the port of New Ross; the equivalent
figure for 1332-3 was only £37. Some of the other major ports were
not so seriously affected but all displayed declines; at Cork, for
example, the returns fell from £400 in 1276-7 to £118 in 1332-3. It
is also noticeable that after the Bruce invasions, there are no further
returns for less important ports such as Youghal, Limerick and those
of Ulster, indicating the general decline in the economic well-being of
the colony.

The factor which Otway-Ruthven considers made any recovery
impossible and which most severely affected the larger boroughs was
the Black Death.[97] The plague first appeared in 1349 in the ports of
Howth and Drogheda and although very little is known about it, its
effects seem to have been both widespread and serious. The only con-

temporary account is that of Friar Clyn who noted that the cities of Dublin and Drogheda were almost destroyed and 'wasted of men'.[98] There is little doubt that mortality was high, particularly amongst the Anglo-Irish town dwellers, although it was probably less so in rural areas. The population of the island may have been almost halved by the plague and there is no doubt that it furthered the decline of most of the boroughs.

Throughout the remainder of the fourteenth century, the colony continued to decline rapidly and by 1430-40 the area of English control was reduced to the counties of Dublin, Meath, Louth and Kildare,[99] the area defined in 1495 by Poyning's 34th Act as the Pale. Many of the smaller boroughs in the area beyond the Pale must have been deserted by this time, or were at least shrunken compared with their former size. Only the larger and better fortified towns such as Cork, Limerick, Galway and Waterford survived as enclaves amongst the Irish.[100] O'Sullivan has described fourteenth- and fifteenth-century Galway as a city-state, a term which conveys the degree of virtual independence which the surviving, although almost certainly shrunken, Norman boroughs possessed at this period.[101]

Hence, at least in terms of longevity, the era of Norman new-town building in Ireland was not noticeably successful. Many of the speculative new boroughs which they founded are now completely deserted. Forth, Co. Carlow, Carrick-on-Slaney, Bannow, Hevey's Island and Clonmines, all in Co. Wexford, are but a few of the examples. Despite these failures, however, the Norman towns which survived the decline of the colony provided a basis for a revival of new-town building which followed the Tudor re-conquest of Ireland in the second half of the sixteenth century. The essential Norman achievement was the introduction of urban settlement to what had been a rural peasant society and it is noticeable that their most important towns have, with few exceptions, survived into the present landscape to be the most important cities and towns of Ireland today.

APPENDIX 1: MEDIEVAL IRISH BOROUGHS

(The grid references, preceded by the sheet numbers, relate to the Irish Ordnance Survey, ½in. to 1 mile (1:126.726) series

County	Borough	Grid Reference		
Antrim	Bushmills	2,	C	940406
	Carrickfergus	5,	J	415875
	Dunmalys	5,	Dc	400025
	Le Coul	Site unknown		
	Le Ford	5,	J	340760
	Porcros (Portrush)	2,	C	859406
Carlow	Carlow	19,	S	722768
	Forth	19,	S	831730
	Leighlin	19,	S	860655
	Tullow	19,	S	852730
Clare	Bunratty	17,	R	453608
Cork	Buttevant	21,	R	541090
	Castlemora	21,	W	566931
	Cloyne	25,	W	918678
	Cork	22,	W	6070
	Douglas	25,	W	710692
	Fayth	25,	Wc	660700
	Kilmaclennan	21,	R	505062
	Kinsale	25,	W	637505
	Mallow	21,	W	561983
	Youghal	22,	X	105780
Down	Blathewyc	5,	J	490740
	Down	9,	J	487446
	Greencastle	9,	J	247114
Dublin	Bray	16,	O	270190
	Clondalkin	16,	O	070313
	Dalkey	16,	O	265274
	Dublin	16,	O	1030
	Lucan	16,	O	032350
	Lusk	13,	O	214546
	Rathcoole	16,	O	020270
	Saggart	16,	O	038267
	Shankill	16,	O	235270
	Swords	13,	O	183468
	Tallaght	16,	O	093277
Galway	Ardrahyn	14,	M	461122
	Athenry	14,	M	503279
	Dunmore	11,	M	509634

County	Borough	Grid Reference		
	Galway	14,	M	298250
	Kilcolgan	14,	M	421178
	Loughrea	14,	M	620166
	Meelick	15,	M	942138
	Portumna	15,	M	853047
Kerry	Ardfert	21,	Q	784208
	Tralee	21,	Q	834146
Kildare	Ardree	16,	S	687925
	Ardscull	16,	S	726977
	Athy	16,	S	685940
	Ballymore-Eustace	16,	N	927102
	Carbry	16,	N	690344
	Castledermot	16,	S	782852
	Clane	16,	N	877278
	Cloncurry	16,	N	803411
	Dunfert	16,	N	777381
	Glassely	16,	S	756982
	Kildare	16,	N	727127
	Kilkea	16,	S	744890
	Leixlip	16,	O	033354
	Moone	16,	S	797923
	Mounmohenek	19,	S	730832
	Naas	16,	N	892192
	Narragh	16,	S	780989
	Oughterard	16,	N	958263
	Rathangen	16,	N	675192
	Rathmore	16,	N	960195
	Straffan	16,	N	909302
	Tipper	16,	N	918185
Kilkenny	Callan	18,	S	413437
	Castletown	18,	S	421273
	Collaghmore	18,	S	421389
	Coyketle	Site unknown		
	Gowran	19,	S	630535
	Inistiogue	19,	S	634378
	New Vill of Jerpoint	19,	S	570403
	Kells	18,	S	493432
	Kilkenny	19,	S	505560
	Kilmanagh	18,	S	391522
	Knocktopher	19,	S	530376
	Odagh	18,	S	457623
	Rosbergen	23,	S	713277
	Thomastown	19,	S	585419
Leix	Castletown	15,	S	341920
	Killaban	16,	S	691857
	New Vill of Leys	16,	S	523980
Limerick	Adare	17,	R	463460
	Ardagh	17,	R	280377
	Carkenlis	18,	R	680493
	Corkmoy	Site unknown		

County	Borough	Grid Reference
	Croom	17, R 513411
	Glenogra	17, R 595149
	Gren	18, R 758437
	Kilmallock	17, R 610276
	Knockany	18, R 682359
	Limerick	17, R 575565
	Mungrett	17, R 544538
	Newtown	Site unknown
Louth	Ardee	13, N 959913
	Carlingford	9, J 190115
	Castlefrank	9, Hc 955036
	Collon	13, N 998822
	Drogheda	13, O 090752
	Nova Villa of Dundalk	9, J 045075
	Castletown Dundalk	9, J 031084
	Louth	9, H 057011
	Roche	9, H 990118
	Termofechin	13, O 142805
Meath	Athboy	13, N 713638
	Colp	13, O 126744
	Drogheda	13, O 090750
	Drumcondra	13, N 886898
	Duleek	13, O 046687
	Greenoge	13, O 096500
	Kells	13, N 741758
	Marninerstown	13, O 133760
	New Town Trim	13, N 814569
	Nobber	13, N 824864
	Ratoath	13, O 020519
	Skreen	13, N 952604
	Slane	13, N 961742
	Siddan	13, N 893848
	Trim	13, N 800568
Roscommon	Ballintobber	12, M 729744
	Rathfernan	Site unknown
	Rindown	12, N 004541
	Roscommon	12, M 876644
Sligo	Sligo	7, G 693359
Tipperary	Ardmayle	18, S 058457
	Athassel	18, S 011365
	Ballincloch	18, R 893749
	Ballyhaghill	18, S 063598
	Carrick-on-Suir	22, S 398215
	Cashel	18, S 077405
	Clonmel	22, S 200226
	Fethard	18, S 207350
	Fetmothan	Site unknown
	Imelach (Emly)	18, R 764348
	Karkeul	Site unknown
	Knockgraffon	18, S 053298

County	Borough	Grid Reference
	Kyldenall	Site unknown
	Lisronagh	18, S 201295
	Lynnane	18, Rc 940400
	Moyallif	18, S 042560
	Nenagh	18, R 867791
	Roscrea	15, S 135893
	Thurles	18, S 131588
	Tipperary	18, R 890358
Waterford	Dungarvan	22, X 260930
	Kilmidan	23, S 513108
	Stradbally	22, X 370978
	Waterford	23, S 605120
Westmeath	Athlone	12, N 040415
	Kilbixy	12, N 322615
	Loxinedy	12, N 210490
Wexford	Bannow	23, S 823072
	Carrick-on-Slaney	23, T 016235
	Clonmines	23, S 843129
	Curtun	Site unknown
	Edermine	23, S 978345
	Ferns	19, T 020498
	Fethard	23, S 792050
	Hervey's Island	23, S 687163
	Mayglass	23, T 015112
	New Ross	23, S 720275
	Old Ross	23, S 799273
	Taghman	23, S 916198
	Wexford	23, T 050215
Wicklow	Arklow	19, T 250730
	Burgage	Site unknown
	Donaghmore	16, S 923941
	Dunlavin	16, N 871015
	Kilmacberne	Site unknown
	Newcastle Mackinegam	16, O 298042
	Wicklow	16, O 315940

APPENDIX 2: MARKET TOWNS

(Settlements which received grants of weekly markets but with no further evidence of borough status.)

County	Market Town	Grid Reference
Clare	Clare	17, R 351741
	Corofin	14, R 285887
Cork	Athnowen	25, W 548699
	Ballinaboy	25, W 634604
	Ballyhac	Site unknown
	Ballyhooley	22, W 728992
	Ballynoe	22, W 932898
	Bridgetown	22, R 670010
	Carrig	Site unknown
	Carrigaline	25, W 729620
	Carrigohan	25, W 615711
	Carrigtohill	22, W 821730
	Castlelyons	22, W 840930
	Castlemartyr	22, W 962732
	Castletown	22, R 683023
	Corkbeg	25, W 840638
	Doneraile	21, R 600073
	Dunbulloge	22, W 688809
	Dundanion	25, W 722719
	Glanworth	22, R 756043
	Grenagh	21, W 579847
	Inishonan	25, W 546571
	Kilworth	22, R 832028
	Mageely	22, W 962757
	Middleton	22, W 880735
	Mitchelstown	22, R 816127
	Rincurran	25, W 653495
	Ringrone	25, W 634466
	Shendon	25, Wc 670750
	Timoleague	25, W 472438
Down	Molendinis in L'Ard	Site unknown
Kildare	Maynooth	16, N 938378
Kilkenny	Aghour	Site unknown
	Clonmore	22, S 487174
	Deravald	Site unknown
Longford	Moydowe	12, N 148687
Louth	Clonmore	13, O 100880
	Dunleer	13, O 058882
Meath	Derevagh	13, N 708786

County	Market Town	Grid Reference
	Dunboyne	13, O 013422
	Killeen	13, N 935550
	Rathkenny	13, N 893773
Tipperary	Actonagh	Site unknown
	Cahir	22, S 050248
	Finnoure	18, S 288167
Waterford	Tallow	22, W 995933
Westmeath	Adleck	Site unknown
	Incheleffer	Site unknown
	Lin	12, N 425498
	Mulingar	12, N 435530
Wexford	Enniscorthy	23, S 974398
	Senebald	19, S 896485

Notes

1. A ring-fort is a circular bank and fosse enclosing a space which contained a farmstead.
2. A clachan is a nucleated settlement with no formal plan, simply consisting of dwelling houses and outhouses.
3. J. O'Donovan (ed.), *Annals of the Kingdom of Ireland by the Four Masters* (Dublin, 1848), II, p. 1050.
4. Ibid., III, p. 693.
5. *Chartae, Privilegia et Immunitates* (Dublin, 1889), p. 10.
6. G. MacNiocaill, *Na Buirgeisi,* 1 (Dublin, 1964), p. 246.
7. R. Caulfield (ed.), *Rotulus Pipae Clonensis* (Cork, 1859), pp. 15-22.
8. *Chartae, Privilegia et Immunitates*, p. 33.
9. A.J. Otway-Ruthven, 'The Character of Norman Settlement in Ireland', *Historical Studies*, V (1965), p. 79.
10. E. Curtis, *A History of Medieval Ireland* (London, 1923), pp. 212-13.
11. R.E. Glasscock, 'Moated Sites and Deserted Boroughs and Villages; Two neglected Aspects of Anglo-Norman Settlement in Ireland', in N. Stephens and R.E. Glasscock (eds.), *Irish Geographical Studies* (Belfast, 1970), p. 171.
12. The medieval Liberty of Meath comprised the present counties of Meath, Westmeath and parts of Longford and Offaly.
13. The medieval Liberty of Leinster comprised the present counties of Wexford, Carlow, Kildare and Kilkenny and parts of Offaly and Leix.
14. The most detailed account of the Norman occupation of Ireland is contained in A.J. Otway-Ruthven, *A History of Medieval Ireland* (London, 1968).
15. The details of the various sub-infeudations are contained in G.H. Orpen, *Ireland under the Normans, 1169-1333,* 4 vols. (Oxford, 1911-20).
16. Ibid., II, p. 172.
17. A motte was a truncated conical mound of earth, this being surmounted with a wooden tower; the bailey was the forecourt of the mount and was generally rectangular in shape.
18. *Cal. Docs. Ireland, 1171-1251*, No. 1401.
19. Ibid., No. 2181.
20. J.T. Gilbert (ed.), *Historical and Municipal Documents of Ireland, AD 1172-1320* (London, 1870), p. XXIV.
21. MacNiocaill, *Na Buirgeisi,* I p. 172.
22. *Chartae, Privilegia et Immunitates,* p. 10.
23. Ibid., p. 10.
24. Ibid., p. 9.
25. MacNiocaill, *Na Buirgeisi,* I, p. 158.
26. Ibid., p. 135.
27. *Chartae, Privilegia et Immunitates*, pp. 16-17.
28. MacNiocaill, *Na Buirgeisi,* 1, p. 130.
29. Orpen, *Ireland under the Normans*, 1, p. 374.
30. P. Gale, *An Inquiry into the Ancient Corporate System of Ireland* (London, 1834), Appendix IV.
31. A.J. Otway-Ruthven, 'The Medieval County of Kildare', *Irish Historical Studies,* XI (1958-9), p. 184.
32. B.J. Graham, 'The Anglo-Norman Settlement Pattern of Eastmeath, 1169-1660', Ph.D. thesis, Queen's University, Belfast, 1972.
33. J. Mills and M.J. McEnery (eds.), *Calendar of the Gormanston Register* (Dublin, 1916), p. 8.
34. *Cal. Justiciary Rolls. Ireland, 1295-1303*, p. 202.
35. *Cal. Docs. Ireland, 1293-1301*, No. 511.

36. *Cal. Justic. Rolls Ireland, 1305-1307*, p. 256.
37. E. Curtis (ed.), *Calendar of Ormond Deeds*, 11 (Dublin, 1934), p. 224.
38. A. Gwynn and R.N. Hadcock, *Medieval Religious Houses, Ireland* (London, 1970), p. 84.
39. Ibid., p. 95.
40. Gilbert, *Historical and Municipal Documents*, p. XXXII.
41. E.M. Carus-Wilson (ed.), *The Overseas Trade of Bristol in the Later Middle Ages* (Bristol, 1937), pp. 180-289.
42. H.C. Darby (ed.), *Historical Geography of England Before 1800.* (Cambridge, 1936), pp. 295-6.
43. *Cal. Docs. Ireland, 1252-1284*, No. 1429. The ports of Ireland are listed as being Rosse (New Ross), Waterford, Wexford, Dublin, Drogheda, Cnakfergus (Carrickfergus), Galvy (Galway), Kork, Youghal and Limerick.
44. Merchants from Bordeaux were dealing with wine in Ireland in 1283, *Cal. Docs. Ireland, 1252-1284*, No. 2127.
45. M.D. O'Sullivan, *Old Galway: the History of a Norman Colony in Ireland* (Cambridge, 1942), p. 31.
46. *Reports of the Deputy Keeper of the Public Records*, 36th Report to the 43th Report (Dublin, 1903-10).
47. Presumably Tralee and Dingle.
48. *Cal. Docs. Ireland, 1293-1301*, No. 253.
49. *Cal. Docs. Ireland, 1252-1284*, No. 2340. The burgess rent of Castledermot was £4.12s.4d. in 1284, equivalent to a burgess household population of approximately 460.
50. J.S. Fleming, *The Town-Wall Fortifications of Ireland* (Paisley, 1914), p. 9.
51. Ibid., p. 45.
52. *Cal. Justic. Rolls Ireland, 1305-1307*, p. 348.
53. W.O'Sullivan, *The Economic History of Cork City from the Earliest Times to the Act of Union* (Cork, 1937), p. 24.
54. *Cal. Docs. Ireland, 1302-1307*, No. 653.
55. S. Lewis, *Topographical Dictionary of Ireland*, II (London, 1837), p. 110.
56. Curtis, *History of Medieval Ireland*, pp. 213-18.
57. *Cal. Justic. Rolls Ireland, 1308-1314*, p. 137.
58. Otway-Ruthven, *Character of Norman Settlement*, p. 80.
59. *Cal. Docs. Ireland, 1302-1307*, No. 617.
60. *Cal. Inquisitions Post Mortem*, V, p. 56.
61. Otway-Ruthven, *Character of Norman Settlement*, p. 80.
62. *Cal. Docs. Ireland, 1302-1307*, No. 667; *Cal. Inquisitions Post Mortem*, IV, p. 329.
63. *Cal. Docs. Ireland, 1252-1284*, No. 1912.
64. Ibid., 1293-13-1. No. 551.
65. Contained in N.B. White (ed.), *The Red Book of Ormond* (Dublin, 1932) and E. Curtis (ed.), *Calendar of Ormond Deeds*, 6 vols. (Dublin, 1932-9).
66. *Cal. Docs. Ireland, 1302-1304*, No. 617.
67. C. McNeill (ed.), *Calendar of Archbishop Alen's Register* (Dublin, 1950), pp. 176-7.
68. Ibid., p. 177.
69. *The Red Book of Ormond*, p. 63.
70. P.H. Hore, *History of the Town and County of Wexford*, 6 vols. (1908-11), IV, p. 190.
71. J.C. Russell, 'Late 13th Century Ireland as a Region', *Demography*, iii (1966), pp. 500-12. There are several errors in Russell's identification of settlements and many of the population figures which he gives are suspect.
72. Ibid., p. 504.

73. B. O'Riordain, Excavations at High Street and Winetavern Street, Dublin',
    Med. Arch., IV (1971), p. 73.
74. *Cal, Docs. Ireland, 1302-1307,* No. 617.
75. Hore, *History of Wexford,* V, p. 102.
76. *38th Report Deputy Keeper,* p. 42.
77. *Cal. Inquisitions Post Mortem,* VI, p. 340.
78. *Cal. Docs. Ireland, 1302-1307,* No. 653.
79. *Cal. Docs. Ireland, 1285-1292,* No. 459.
80. Ibid. There were 226 burgages at Bunratty in 1288.
81. *Cal. Inquisitions Post Mortem,* VIII, p. 121. The burgage rent of Nenagh
    was £11.14s. in 1339.
82. *Red Book of Ormond,* p. 45. The burgage rent of Thurles was £11.8s.7d. in
    1303.
83. H.T. Knox, 'Occupation of Connaught by the Anglo-Normans after AD
    1237', *J. Roy, Soc. Antiq. Ireland,* XXXII (1902), p. 397. The burgage rent
    of Galway was £11.6s. in 1333.
84. Orpen, *Ireland under the Normans,* 1, pp. 373-93.
85. Carlow had a burgess household population of over 800 in 1307, *Cal. Docs.
    Ireland, 1302-1307,* No. 617; Kildare had a burgess household population
    of about 945 in 1331, G. MacNiocail (ed.), *The Red Book of the Earls of
    Kildare* (Dublin, 1964), No. 31.
86. *Cal. Justic. Rolls Ireland, 1305-1307,* p. 29.
87. *43rd Report Deputy Keeper,* p. 39.
88. *Cal. Docs. Ireland, 1302-1307,* No. 617.
89. *Red Book of Ormond,* p. 28.
90. *Cal. Docs. Ireland, 1252-1284,* No. 2340.
91. Otway-Ruthven, *History of Medieval Ireland,* p. 223.
92. *38th Report Deputy Keeper,* p. 42.
93. *Cal. Docs. Ireland, 1302-1307,* No. 666.
94. *Cal. Inquisitions Post Mortem,* VI, pp. 326-7.
95. MacNeill (ed.), *Cal. of Alen's Register,* pp. 195-6.
96. G.H. Orpen, 'The Earldom of Ulster', *J. Roy. Soc. Antiq. Ireland,* III
    (sixth series) (1913), pp. 133-43.
97. Otway-Ruthven, *History of Medieval Ireland,* p. 267.
98. A. Gwyn, 'The Black Death in Ireland', *Studies,* XXIV (1935), p. 27.
99. Curtis, *History of Medieval Ireland,* p. 301.
100. Otway-Ruthven, *History of Medieval Ireland,* p. 369.
101. O'Sullivan, *Old Galway,* p. 37.

3 IRISH TOWNS IN THE SIXTEENTH AND SEVENTEENTH CENTURIES

R.A. Butlin

Introduction

Among the many variables which conditioned urban development in
Ireland in the two centuries that mark the transition from the late
medieval to the early modern period, the political relations between
England and Ireland almost certainly rank first in order of significance.
Successive changes in English policies for Ireland, starting with that of
Henry VIII and ending, perhaps, with the Williamite confiscations,
affected both directly and indirectly the fortunes of those Irish towns
and cities which had their origins in earlier centuries, and also affected
the creation of a network of new towns, and thus established, at least
in a locational sense, the roots of the modern urban system of Ireland.
These policies reflect the changing perception by successive English
monarchs, governments and administrators of the role of Ireland not
only in the English but also in the European political, religious, social
and economic system. The wider European context is significant, for
Ireland's well-established trading links with the countries of western
Europe ensured the continued development and relative prosperity of
the port towns of Ireland. In addition, the Catholicism of the majority
of the population meant that 'as the religious animosities of the post-
Reformation era developed, an unconquered Ireland was increasingly
feared as a spear-head of the Counter-Reformation',[1] and the country
thus became involved in the political and territorialist intrigues arising
from the religious antipathies of Europe. The broad context of Irish
urban development in the sixteenth and seventeenth centuries is therefore related to the beginnings of the Western imperial era and the
expansion of the European state system, the latter associated with the
increasing centralisation of government and administration, greater
interest in the wealth and power of the state and therefore in the
'expansion of Europe' via the extension of imperial political and
commercial networks over very large areas of the globe. England's
'micro-imperialist' policy towards Ireland is in some respects a micro-
cosm of the 'macro-imperialism' which she and other western European
countries formulated and implemented in respect of New World
colonies.

61

Imperialism, in its various forms, has strong links with the process of urbanisation. Sjoberg, for example, has hypothesised 'that the patterns of urban development, dissemination and decline result mainly from like changes in the political (or power) structure on the societal level — especially the rise and fall of empires',[2] suggesting that the most highly developed political systems in any particular period create the most highly developed urban complexes and more intensive kinds of commercial activity (as a result of the creation of a high degree of social and political stability). He stresses the role of cities for sustaining hegemony in newly won territories, their administrative role in the organisation of territory as a viable political entity, and their function as 'media through which the ruling order has exploited the fruits of conquest'.[3] His central theme is the dependence of urban living on the vagaries of political power, to which may be attributed both the rise and decline of towns and cities.[4] A necessary rider to this theorem is the variable effect of the size of the territorial base controlled by the political system, for size can affect the diversity of resources for urban existence, and relatively small and poorly endowed areas can only, in many instances, achieve urban prominence by drawing upon the resources of a larger area — the dependence of the Greek city-states on the Mediterranean region as a whole is a good example, as also, perhaps, is that of the port towns of Ireland. Many facets of this hypothesis on the rise and fall of cities can be illustrated by the Irish towns of the period under consideration.

Irish Towns in the Early Sixteenth Century

The towns of Ireland in the early sixteenth century comprised the surviving remnants (and somewhat precariously surviving remnants in some cases) of the urban system which had been developed during the Anglo-Norman colonisation, which lasted effectively from the twelfth to the early fourteenth century. The urban network thus developed was based on pre-existing urban or proto-urban nodes, specifically in the form of monastic and church sites, Viking settlements, castles and other strongholds. The regional variations of the Anglo-Norman urban system have been described in the previous chapter, and it was a weakened form of this urban system which formed the main urban pattern of Ireland in the early sixteenth century. The weakening of the Anglo-Norman colony and lordships had been precipitated in the fourteenth and fifteenth centuries by a variety of causes, including Edward Bruce's invasion, the migration of Anglo-Norman families back to England, a process of 'hibernicisation' of many that remained, plague, bad harvests

Figure 5: Location map

and a general Gaelic resurgence, and was inevitably accompanied by the decline and decay of many of the smaller towns, some of which had been little more than notional boroughs. Others, though with the physical and legal attributes of urban status — walls and charters — were unable to survive as economic entities.

In the late Middle Ages there was, in fact, a marked reduction of English interest in Ireland, because of the involvement of political and military energy in the French Wars and the Wars of the Roses. The former policy of encouraging colonisation, particularly in the vicinity of the highly anglicised area of the Pale, around Dublin, and in other densely colonised areas, was replaced by one which sought simply to maintain a much-shrunken Pale, which had become 'little more than a foothold upon the island, the shrivelled beach-head of a once ambitious conquest'.[5] This retreat to a defensive colonial policy is clearly shown by the Statutes of Kilkenny of 1366, which were intended to maintain English law and customs in the more loyal areas, and in which reference is made to the effects of native Irish traders on the decline of some of the older 'colony' towns, with consequent (but ineffective) regulations prohibiting trade with the Irish. The major towns of Ireland in the late Middle Ages were, therefore, those which operated successfully both as ports and as market centres for large hinterlands. The isolation of most of the ports from both London and Dublin gave them a high degree of autonomy, and their position has been likened to that of the early city-states of Europe. Thus W.F.T. Butler states that:

In those countries the want of a strong central government soon taught the inhabitants of the cities, set round as they were with powerful enemies, to look after themselves, and to establish a local government that soon passed into virtual independence. In France, Spain, and England, each with a strong central government, no such thing was possible; but in Ireland, where for two centuries (from 1300 to 1500 A.D.) the royal power was merely nominal, the English colonies left to themselves developed very much on Continental lines; and so we find the townsmen of Galway and Limerick, and in a less degree of Cork and Waterford, acting with a degree of freedom from outside control, to which the citizens of London or Bristol never attained, and which in some measure approximates as far as the poverty of the land would allow, to the great development of civic independence in the municipalities of Italy and Central Europe.[6]

The rise of a system of city-states is the natural outcome, according to at least one theory of economic history,[7] of the development of a mercantile economy, based initially on the expansion of external trade, and associated with the emergence of groups of merchants or traders. The reason for the importance of the 'city-state' phase in European history is, according to Hicks, 'mainly geographical',[8] in that 'the Mediterranean has been outstanding as a highway of contact, between countries of widely different productive capacities; further, it is rich in pockets and crannies, islands, promontories, and valleys, which in the same conditions have been readily defensible.'[9] The role of the Irish Sea and the Atlantic Ocean has most certainly been similar in character, in relation to Ireland, to that of the Mediterranean in relation to Europe. Trade between Ireland and the countries of western Europe dates back to prehistory, but the development of a mercantile economy, based principally on the ports of the south and east of Ireland, effectively dates to the thirteenth century, and reached a peak in the fifteenth and sixteenth centuries. In the sixteenth century England's Irish trade was principally conducted by the ports of Chester (and Liverpool) and Bristol, and the customs accounts of the period give a picture of the nature and size of the trade.[10] Ireland's major exports were primary products, particularly fish, animal hides, skins, wool, linen, linen yarn and timber, and her major imports were wine, iron and salt. The significance of each of these commodities to the trading activities varied between the ports, but the aggregate effect of their continued export and import was to give to the merchants of the port towns profits which were quite considerable in the context of the generally low standards of living of the majority of the Irish people, and thus create an air of urban prosperity, reflected in the substantial town houses of the merchants in places like Galway, Cork, Waterford and Wexford.

Trade was mainly channelled through the ports of the south of the country, the area where natural configuration — drowned river estuaries and a highly indented coastline — and position in relation to Britain and France and Spain, offered the most advantageous conditions for successful mercantile activity. The merchants involved in trade were generally members of old merchant families, many of which had been in Ireland since the period of Anglo-Norman colonisation. Some came from families which had migrated into the towns at the time of the Gaelic resurgence in the fourteenth and fifteenth centuries, and others were of Gaelic origin (there having been, in some parts of Ireland, a well-established tradition of Irish merchants operating in inland areas, selling imported goods and buying various commodities for export).[11]

The most important port towns of the south coast of Ireland were
Cork and Waterford. Cork is shown in early maps as an oval-shaped
town located on a heavily defended site in the River Lee, features
described by Camden later in the century:

> It is of an oval form, enclosed with walls, and encompassed with
> the chanel of the river, which also crosses it, and it is not accessible
> but by bridges; lying along as it were in one direct street, with a
> bridge over it.[12]

Cork was small in area, but a populous and wealthy trading city,
probably smaller in size than Waterford and Limerick. In early Tudor
times it was described as the fourth city of Ireland, and the advantages
of its excellent harbour were frequently noted. In spite of the land-
based hostility from Irish neighbours, and the maritime aggression of
both English and Irish privateers and pirates, the merchants of Cork
prospered, and constantly sought renewal of their charters of privilege
and incorporation from the Crown in order to maximise the profit-
ability of their activities by retaining a high degree of monopoly. Its
hinterland was extensive, and the city had strong trading links with the
ports of south-west England, notably Bristol, and of Flanders, France
and Spain.

Waterford was an extremely important port city, whose location on
Waterford harbour provided it with a very large hinterland, access to
which was afforded by the rivers Suir, Nore and Barrow: 'the seat of it
be commodious . . . by reason that so many inland shires are served
from thence where the navigable rivers of that part do join and fall into
the sea.'[13] Waterford was probably the second-largest and second-
wealthiest city of Ireland in the early sixteenth century. Export of cloth
and skins went to England and the Continent, and many of Ireland's
imports were distributed from Waterford. Like Cork, Waterford was in an
important fishing area, and Waterford vessels were also active in deep-
sea fishing. In form, Waterford was described later in the century, as
'properly builded, and very well compact', with 'thick buildings and
narrow streets'.[14] The prosperity of the merchants of Waterford was
thought by the citizens of some of the east coast port towns, notably
Dublin, Drogheda and Dundalk, to derive from privileges granted to
Waterford (and to Limerick and Youghal) by Henry VIII in the form of
fee farms, customs and poundages, which enabled the merchants to
charge very low customs rates to foreign merchants who, therefore, it

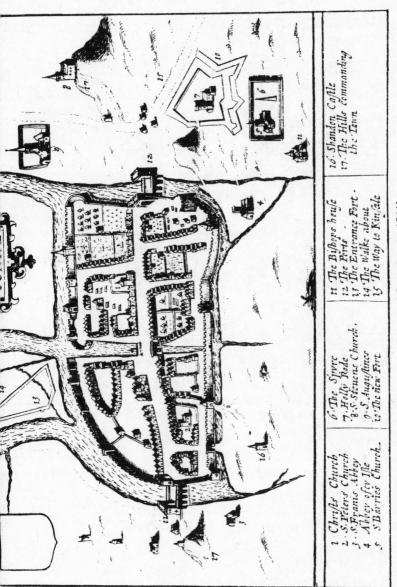

1. Chrifts Church
2. S. Peters Church
3. S. Francis Abbey
4. Abbey of ev IJle
5. S Barries Church.

6. The Spyre
7. Holly Rode
8. S. Steuens Church.
9. S. Auguftines
10. The new Fort

11. The Biſhops houſe
12. The Ports
13. The Entrance Fort
14. The Walks about
15. The Way to Kinſale

16. Shandon Caſtle
17. The Hills commanding
    the Town

Figure 6: Cork c. 1610 (John Speed, Theatre of the Empire of Great Britain, 1611)

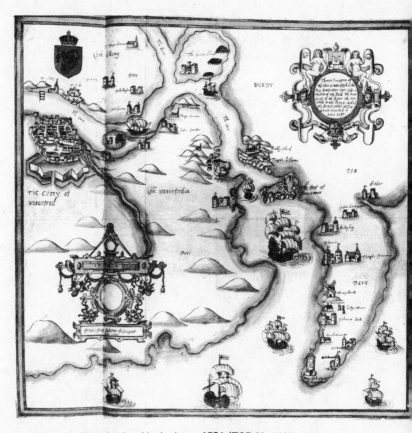

Figure 7: Waterford and its harbour, 1591 (TCD Ms 1209 no. 64)

was claimed, tended to patronise Waterford, 'to the intent to have all resort of merchant strangers to themselves, knowing thereby to have their merchandizes the better cheap at their wills'.[15] Thus, 'the English citizens of Dublin, Drogheda, Dundalk and the four obeysant shires' were rendered 'destitute of salt, wine, iron, and other merchandize which is brought from abroad',[16] and forced to buy their goods from the merchants of Waterford. It may well be that the privileges enjoyed by Waterford were considered, by its citizens, to be no more than just reward for their consistent loyalty to the English Crown throughout the late Middle Ages, a loyalty which had propagated constant conflict with the Irish populace in surrounding areas.

The other port towns of the south coast included Youghal, Dungarvon, Kinsale and Baltimore. Youghal, a small walled town on the Blackwater, had developed as a seaport after the Anglo-Norman colonisation, importing wine, salt, manufactured goods and iron, and exporting salmon, cloth and timber in various forms.[17] Dungarvon was of modest size and significance only, whereas Kinsale, which had received its first charter in 1333, was a major fishing port, fishing being an important activity along the south coast west of Cork harbour, both for Irish and foreign fishermen. Kinsale was linked to the Cork's port functions, and acted as a kind of entrepôt and outport, but had independent trading links with Britain, notably through Bristol, France and Spain. Baltimore was also a fishing port.

The greatest density of port towns in Ireland was in the south, but there were, of course, significant port towns elsewhere. The most important was Dublin, the centre of the Pale, and the largest city in Ireland, described by travellers in euphoric terms at various times in the sixteenth century as 'the beauty and eye of Ireland'[18] and 'the Royal City of Ireland, its most notable mart and chief seat of justice, defended with strong walls, adorned with beautiful buildings and well peopled with inhabitants'.[19] Dublin was the main stronghold of the English administration in Ireland, and the key settlement of the Pale, fulfilling many urban functions including the administration of government, law and justice, manufacturing activities and a wide range of services (many of which were controlled by merchant guilds) and trade. Dublin's trade was mainly with Chester and Liverpool, and the port served a large hinterland, including much of Leinster and large areas of Ulster with which, in many cases, contact was by sea. The functioning of the port was somewhat handicapped by the presence of the bar at Ringsend, where the main port area was then located: 'The only fault of this city', wrote Stanihurst, 'is that it is less frequented of merchant strangers, because of the bare [barred] haven.'[20] Nevertheless Dublin was the most important of the ports on the east coast, and retained this position throughout the whole of the sixteenth and seventeenth centuries, having little contact with the ports of south-west England, but gradually increasing trade with Chester and Liverpool. The city itself appears in Elizabethan maps as a compact medieval city, trapezoidal in form with strong walls and fortifications, with the River Liffey forming its effective northern limit and Dublin Castle its main stronghold. Dublin was an important ecclesiastical centre, and at the time of the Dissolution there were in the city a large number of religious establishments, including two cathedrals, eleven parish churches and a variety of hospitals, almshouses, friaries, abbeys and nunneries. Their influence extended outside the city to their extensive properties in the Pale, notably in County Dublin.

The other east coast port towns were not as large as Dublin, though Drogheda, later described as 'the best town in Ireland, and truly not far behind some of their cities',[21] rivalled Dublin in the value of goods exported to Chester and Liverpool. Dundalk, with 'the privilege of a good haven', Carlingford, Arklow and Wicklow were port towns of lesser significance. Wexford, on the estuary of the river Slaney, was a major fishing port and timber exporter.[22] Large quantities of fish were exported to England from Ireland in the sixteenth century, notwithstanding the activities of French and Spanish fishing vessels in the Irish fishing grounds.[23]

The major port towns of the west coast of Ireland were Galway, Limerick and Sligo. Galway was, from its foundation by the Norman De Burgos in the thirteenth century to the sixteenth century, one of the most isolated towns in Ireland, and thus

for three hundred years it was virtually an independent city-state, self-contained politically and ecclesiastically, being obliged to rely on its own resources for its very existence since it was so completely cut off from the English central authority at Dublin.[24]

Galway, on account of her key site and loyalty, was known as the 'Key to all Connaught', and her economic health and vitality epitomised her political significance. Since early medieval times, the merchant families or 'tribes' of Galway had promoted trade with Britain and western Europe, notably France, Portugal and Andalusia, and had made trade contacts with the Irish of Connaught and with the inhabitants of Clare Island and the Aran Islands. One of the most important

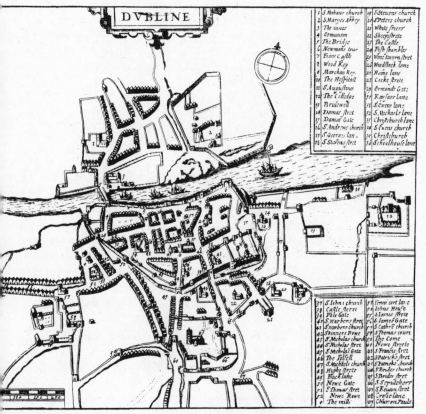

Figure 8: Dublin, c. 1610 (John Speed, *Theatre of the Empire of Great Britain,* 1611)

commodities imported by the merchants of Galway was wine, and they
exported fish, hides, leather, wool, grain and timber. The wealth of
Galway's merchants was reflected in the churches, town houses, and
castles of the town. The city was described by Camden as being

> neat and fair-built with firm stone, of an oval form, and somewhat
> tower-like; famous for a Bishop's See and by reason of its harbour
> . . . well frequented by merchants, and enriched by a great trade in
> all sorts of commodities both by sea and land,[25]

and by Campion as 'a proper neat citie at seasyde'.[26] Galway, like the
other main port towns of Ireland, was strongly fortified by walls, which
had been completed by the end of the fourteenth century, and in the
sixteenth century, during the increasing instability of Ireland's political
failures, further attempts were made to strengthen its fortifications.[27]
Galway received a new charter in 1545, which confirmed earlier privileges and also added a substantial number of new ones. Galway was,
for example, freed from several tolls and from the prisage of wine, and
allowed to export all types of goods and merchandise. Attempts were
made, quite illegally, to prevent merchants from Limerick, Cork,
Waterford and other places coming by ship to Galway with goods and
trading there:[28] although unsuccessful, these attempts were symbolic
of the jealousy guarded near-autonomy of Galway and the other port
towns.

Limerick, a 'fayre walled cittie', was large and well populated, with
the advantage of a location on the Shannon estuary, the 'very main sea'
being 'three score miles distant from the town, and yet the river is so
navigable as a ship of 200 tons may sail to the quay of the city'.[29] It
was a major port, trading with France and particularly with Spain and
Portugal. Limerick had a rich hinterland, with important salmon
fisheries on the Shannon. The site of Limerick occupied both banks and
an island of the river Shannon at the head of its estuary. By the fifteenth century it had been extensively fortified and it was one of the
most strongly fortified towns in Ireland. That part of the town which
developed on King's Island was known as the English town or the High
Town, opposite to which, to the south-east, was the Irish town, on the
river bank, the two sectors of the town being clearly distinguished on
contemporary maps.[30]

Sligo was possibly the only example in Ireland of an Anglo-Norman
borough which continued its existence in the Middle Ages under the
control of a Gaelic lord.[31] Sligo stands at the head of Sligo Bay, which

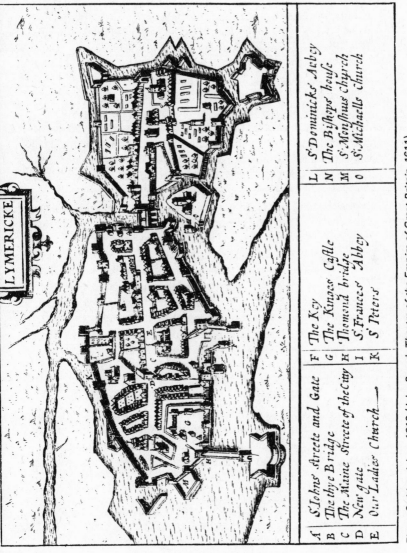

LYMERICKE

A   S. Johns streete and Gate
B   The thye Bridge
C   The Maine Streete of the Citty
D   New gate
E   Our Ladies Church ⟶

F   The Key
G   The Kinges Castle
H   Thomond bridge
I   S. Frances Abbey
K   S. Peters

L   S. Dominicks Arbey
N   The Bishops house
M   S. Monshus church
O   S. Michaells church

Figure 9: Limerick, c. 1610 (John Speed, *Theatre of the Empire of Great Britain*, 1611)

is fed by rivers whose valleys give access to the interior of what are now counties Sligo and Leitrim. From the date of the foundation of Sligo Castle — 1245 — to the fourteenth century, Sligo's functions had been primarily military and ecclesiastical, but with the Gaelic resurgence and the activities of local Irish merchants it had doubled as a significant port, with herrings being a major export item.[32]

The largest inland town in Ireland in the sixteenth century was undoubtedly Kilkenny. Located on the banks of the river Nore, Kilkenny developed after the Norman invasion as a major centre of Anglo-Norman influence in Ireland in a region of dense Norman colonisation. A walled town with a large castle, Kilkenny developed as a major trading town and centre of manufacture and processing. The *Liber Primus Kilkenniensis*, the common book of the town, compiled between *c.* 1352 and 1537, affords much detail of the form and the life of the town.[33] The range of occupations was extensive, for references are made to labourers, bakers, tailors, shoemakers, fullers, ale-wives, brewers, merchants, fishermen, cordwainers, dyers, glove-makers, tanners, carpenters, weavers, masons, butchers, cooks, clerks, and a host of borough officials. The operations of these trades were carefully regulated by the customs and statutes of the town, as laid down by the sovereign (the chief officer of the town), the council and the portreeves. The importance of the oligarchic form of control by the sovereign and council and its relation to the English Crown is indicated by the oaths of the town's officials. The sovereign's oath, taken at Michaelmas, required that he should be

> faithful and true to our sovereign lord king Henry VIII that now is, and to his heirs, kings of England and of this realm of Ireland, and to the burgesses of this town, and faithfully shall maintain and defend the laws, statutes, jurisdiction, franchises and liberties of the same.[34]

The statutes of the town contain frequent reference to the necessity for deterring 'foreign' traders and craftsmen from operating in it. Thus in 1530, it was enacted by the sovereign, burgesses and commons of Kilkenny, 'that no inhabitant of the town shall allow or permit any manner of man to buy or sell any kind of merchandise within his house or houses', and

> by the same authority it is established, ordained and enacted that no merchant in the town shall receive any foreign craftsman or his son

in his service to be instructed or informed in that craft, or receive any of them to be apprenticed to the said craft, on pain of 100s.[35]

It is clear from the town book that the control of the town was very much the prerogative of a small number of merchant families, whose names appear with great frequency in the lists of sovereigns and council members: Roth, Archer, Shee, Sherlock, Haked and FitzLawrence, for example.

The necessity of the upkeep of the defences of Kilkenny and the maintenance of the military skills of its inhabitants is a constant theme in the town's records. In 1517, for example, new stone doors were constructed on the eastern side of the tolsell (town hall) and an iron grating erected (which the sovereign and community of Kilkenny had 'violently carried off' from the castle of an Irish chieftain in Ossory), and 'several guns were made, and divers hauberks bought for the inhabitants of the town for their defence'.[36] In the year 1508 the sovereign ordained 'that every inhabitant of the town of Kilkenny who did not know how to shoot should have a good gleave at his own expense for his own defence and the credit and profit of the town'.[37] Kilkenny's garrison functions are evidenced by the recorded presence of soldiers in the town. In contrast, Kilkenny was also an important ecclesiastical centre, with a cathedral, built on the site of a sixth-century church, and a large number of churches and religious houses.

There was no other inland town in Ireland that approximated to Kilkenny's size or importance. In the areas which had experienced strong colonisation after the Anglo-Norman invasion there survived some smaller walled towns, such as Ardee, Navan, Athboy, Mullingar, Trim, Naas, New Ross, Fethard, Clonmel, Kilmallock and Athenry, which were active centres of trade with their immediate hinterlands and with the larger port cities. It has been suggested that 'the only urban centres in the Gaelic areas were the episcopal towns, such as Armagh and Rosscarbery (which in 1517 was a walled town containing 200 houses), and Cavan, 'the only known example of what could be called town development in a Gaelic lordship'.[38] These smaller inland towns which had endeavoured to maintain their allegiance to the English Crown were certainly the most vulnerable to the vicissitudes of political change, for in spite of the frequent attempts to minimise contact with the native Irish, the facts of geography had to be faced, as had been indicated in a statute of 1463, which stated that 'the profit of every market, city and town in this land depends principally on the resort of Irish people bringing their merchandise to the said cities and towns'.[39]

The fate of some of these smaller towns depended to a large extent on the maintenance of contacts with the larger port towns, of whose 'satellite' hinterland they formed a part, and also on the preservation of peace and peaceable relations with the Irish in their immediate environs. This latter relationship was, at best, tenuous and potentially volatile, as the political upheavals of the second half of the century were to demonstrate, resulting in the progressive and frequent devastation of the inland towns by the Irish. Natural forces also took their toll of some of the older coastal settlements founded by the Normans: two of the earliest corporate towns in Ireland, Bannow and Clonmines — on the south coast of Wexford — had by the seventeenth century become deserted settlements on account of the changes experienced on a pro-grading shoreline. Clonmines had been

> a place of great trade in times past and a harbour for shipping of indifferent bulk until the sand filled up the passage at the ancient town of Bannow at the mouth of the harbour, which was the destruction of both towns.[40]

The towns of Ireland in the first half of the sixteenth century thus exhibited a number of common and distinguishing features. They were generally peripherally distributed, with the port towns being related to groups of satellite towns in the interior. The port towns were the largest towns, and were part of a western European trading system, but they also maintained a high degree of autonomy and of allegiance to the English Crown, notwithstanding the necessity for trading with the Irish inhabitants in their immediate hinterlands. The isolation from other towns and from England, a reflection of the poor inland communications and the barrier posed by the Irish Sea, made them virtually city-states, and conditioned their frequent reliance on the sea as a means of communication with coastal towns. Many of the towns were strongly fortified — there were about 43 walled towns in Ireland at this time — and kept in a near-constant state of alert. Control was mainly vested in small groups of prosperous merchants, whose prosperity was reflected in the impressive houses which they built and inhabited. Urban prosperity, however, such as it was, which had undoubtedly increased in the fifteenth and sixteenth centuries, was severely affected by the political and military upheavals which Ireland experienced in the late sixteenth and early seventeenth centuries — a critical and crucial period in Irish urban history, which witnessed wild fluctuations in the fortunes of the older towns, and the attempted development of a network of new towns designed to effect the pacification of England's troublesome and dangerous neighbour.

The Plantations and Urban Development *c*. 1540-1641

In the year 1541 Henry VIII was declared 'King of Ireland' by the Irish Parliament, meeting in Dublin. This was a symbolic event marking the beginning of a period of increasing English influence and regal authority in Ireland. The adoption of this title came shortly after the suppression of the rebellion of Thomas Fitzgerald ('Silken Thomas'), son of the Earl of Kildare, and the dissolution of the Irish monasteries. Henry's new title, it has been suggested, 'matched his Irish ambition better than the medieval title, Lord of Ireland, which his royal predecessors had borne. And it was a natural step for one who had broken with Rome to take.'[41] His ambition to unify and pacify Ireland, and make that country more strategically reliable had, however, to be tempered by reality: specifically, by the recognition that the substantial power of the Anglo-Irish families and the Gaelic lords outside the Pale and its environs could not be controlled by military conquest and control alone, but by means of a policy which embraced both coercive and conciliatory measures. An example of the latter was the policy of surrender and re-grant, whereby a number of the Gaelic lords who held lands under Irish custom surrendered them to the Crown and were re-granted them under feudal tenancies, though these transactions hardly engendered a long-lived spirit of Anglophilia in the recipients, and largely failed to achieve the envisaged objectives. The 'amiable' and 'good and discrete persuasions' used in Henry's reign to 'bring the Irish lords to further obedience',[42] and which had been accompanied by expeditionary raids by the lord deputies, continued in the reigns of Edward VI, Queen Mary and Queen Elizabeth, with the specific objective of strengthening the area of the Pale and its environs. This was a strategically important objective, for the western borders of the Pale, in Leinster, were continually subject to attack, notably by the O'Connors and the O'Mores. These guerrilla activities were aided by 'fastnesses' (heaths, woods and bogs) of the south midlands, through which ran escape and ambush routes, constructed by the Irish, and in the attempts to suppress such activities, first by conquest and fortifications and subsequently by attempted 'planting' of English settlers, lay the origins of the first of the 'plantations' of Ireland.

(i) Leix and Offaly

After a series of military campaigns against the O'Mores and the

Plantations

Leix and Offaly (1556-)

Munster (1586-)

Antrim and Down (c.1550-)

Ulster (1609-)

Wexford (1611-)

Longford and Leitrim (1618-)

Period of foundation

Norse settlements ●

Norman towns ○

0   kilometres   100

Dates of incorporation

1567 ▢

1610 ◉

1612-13 ⊗

1629 ⊠

other settlements referred to in text   *

Figure 10: Urban foundations in the sixteenth and seventeenth centuries

O'Connors, the fortification called Fort Governor was erected in 1546 on the site of Fort Daingean – a native fort in Offaly, built in the centre of a great marsh, which had been captured. A new fort, Fort Protector, was also erected in the O'More country of Leix. Both of these forts, together with Athlone, formed a triangle of garrisons to the west of the Pale, and it was anticipated that security and unification with the Pale would ensue. By 1557, on account of the failure of this attempt, the increasing impatience of statesmen in England and Ireland with the rebellious Irish, and the cost of maintaining these enclaves, it was decided that further pacification could be achieved by settling more English colonists in the areas around the forts (a process which had already been initiated by the Lord Deputy, Sir Edward Bellingham, during the time of Edward VI). To do so, land had to be confiscated, by means of the shiring of the region, which established the Crown's title and right of confiscation. Under an Act of 1556 the territories were shired, with the O'More territory of Leix becoming Queen's County, and the O'Connor territory of Offaly becoming King's County. The fort in Leix was renamed Maryborough (after the queen), and the fort in Offaly, Philipstown (after her husband). Under the plantation scheme some Irish were expelled and settlers introduced, and Maryborough (whose modern name is Portlaoise) and Philipstown (now Daingean) were given first the status of market towns (in 1567) and later, in 1569, given borough status, with the right to send representatives to Parliament. The plantation was hardly a success, for the dispossessed Irish made frequent attempts to regain their land and the new 'towns' did not develop real urban size and functions until the seventeenth and eighteenth centuries. Nevertheless, the Leix and Offaly plantation attempt initiated a process of colonisation and urbanisation which gathered momentum in the later sixteenth and early seventeenth centuries.

(ii) Munster

During the reign of Elizabeth attempts were made to continue early Tudor policy of control by conciliation in preference to coercion. These attempts involved different kinds of locational policy, as J.H. Andrews has indicated:

> Firstly there were suggestions for extending the network of administrative areas inherited from the middle ages. When rebellion showed this policy to have been ineffective, it gave way to preoccupations about the placing of forts, garrisons and patrols. And when a purely

military régime began to seem intolerably expensive, attention
shifted to the idea of self-sufficient colonies. This progression was
not so much a single orderly sequence of events as a cycle of ideas
that repeated itself obsessively without ever fully being translated into fact. As ideas, the three topics were to some degree inextricable:
local government reform was linked with the making of new towns,
and civil plantations would probably need to be protected by
soldiers.[43]

These topics were evident in the Leix and Offaly plantation, and
became more evident in the case of the Elizabethan plantations, of
which the Munster plantation was the most ambitious. Munster, — the
southernmost of the Irish provinces, had been a restless state throughout the greater part of the sixteenth century, largely on account of the
aggressiveness and internecine struggles of the two great Anglo-Irish
earldoms of Desmond and Ormond. The sixteenth earl of Desmond
had been allowed to return in 1564 from England in the hope that this
would pacify the province, but his return had the opposite effect, and
Desmond was removed from the earldom in 1567. While he was a
prisoner in London the province revolted in response to rumours of
administrative reform, the appearance of English adventurers, and fears
of the suppression of Catholicism. The rebellion waned in 1569, and
was ruthlessly terminated by military action. The Munster rebels were
attainted in 1570, and a President of Munster appointed in 1571. The
new presidency failed to pacify the province, however, and a second
Desmond rebellion took place between 1579 and 1583, a regional
manifestation of the religious antipathies of Europe, with the Desmond
faction acting as defender of the Catholic faith. As before, assistance
was sought and given from Spain, but this was crushed in 1580, and the
rebellion finally suppressed in 1583.

Munster, by the end of the second rebellion, had suffered severe
devastation, and was deemed to be ripe for plantation. In the 1570s a
number of new policies were considered for Ireland, including the
possibility of extensive plantations, and abortive attempts were made
at the plantation of Ulster by private entrepreneurs and adventurers.
This marked a departure from the policy of the Leix and Offaly plantation, which had involved government enterprise and government
resources. The noted parsimony of the Elizabethan administration
favoured the use of private enterprise as a means of advancing the
'risk capital' necessary for the promotion of plantation schemes
intended to effect the pacification of Ireland. The policy of using the

plantation of colonies in alien territories as a means of achieving political stability at low cost, with attendant strategic and economic advantages, was not, of course, new: D.B. Quinn has suggested, in fact, that
'Machiavelli, the most acute of Renaissance political thinkers, had some
influence, though how much it is still impossible to say, on the formu-
lation of the concepts of the Munster plantation',[44] in the sense that
Machiavelli's *Prince*, which cited Roman precedents for colonisation
theories, had been used in the preparation of one of the propagandist
tracts for the plantation of Munster.

In 1586 a scheme 'for the repeopling and inhabiting the Province
of Munster in Ireland', was approved by the queen and government in
London, superseding an earlier plan of 1585. The new scheme provided
for the division of the confiscated areas, amounting to 574,000 acres in
counties Cork, Kerry, Limerick and Waterford, into 20 seigniories of
12,000 'profitable' English acres each, which could be divided into
blocks of *c*. 4,000 acres. The seigniory was conceived as a large square
area 'that was to serve as both manor and parish for a carefully adjusted
cross-section of rural society',[45] with the central village of a block of
seigniories possibly being given the status and functions of a market
town. The notional scheme for a hierarchy of central places to serve the
new colonists was not achieved in practice, for the Munster plantation
in general 'is an excellent example of the ideas of a sixteenth century
government outrunning its capacity for performance'.[46] Many factors
contributed to the failure to achieve full implementation of the initial
plans: difficulties of obtaining accurate surveys, lack of an adequate
regional administrative machinery and infrastructure, difficulty of
attracting sufficient numbers of settlers, and the problem of the removal
of those Irish whose lands had been declared forfeit. In spite of the
attraction of a number of prominent Englishmen and Welshmen as
'undertakers' (who 'undertook' to implement plantation in the areas
which they had been granted, using their own capital) such as Edmund
Spenser, Sir Walter Raleigh and Sir William Herbert, and the immigration of settlers from such counties as Dorset, Somerset, Devon,
Lancashire, Cheshire, Essex, Hampshire and Pembroke, the plantation
fell far short, in its initial stages, of its intended aims of an expected
total planted population somewhere in the region of 8,400. By about
1590, however, the planter population appears to have increased, and
by 1598 it has been estimated that the total planter population may
have reached 12,000 to 15,000 (though the estimate would appear to be
a generous one).[47]

In the early stages of the plantations, settlement was sparse and widely scattered, an inherent strategic weakness which the rising of 1598 clearly demonstrated, but was sufficient to generate exports of primary products such as grain and cattle products and also of timber, via the ports of Munster to south-west England. The older towns of Munster had suffered badly during the second rebellion, and efforts were devoted to their reparation, but with little success until the end of the 1598 rising. The port towns like Youghal, Cork and Limerick acted as refuges for the settlers during the rising, with many others leaving by ship to return to England. Renewed attempts at settlement were made from 1603 to 1642, with some conspicuous successes.

One of the most impressive adventurers and entrepreneurs of the whole Munster plantation was Richard Boyle, who had begun to acquire estates in Munster before 1598, but who in 1603-4 acquired Raleigh's land in Munster, amounting to 42,000 acres in Cork, Waterford and Tipperary. By 1622 he held seven seigniories. In 1620 he became Earl of Cork. Boyle was one of the few adventurers who recognised the necessity for establishing and maintaining an urban network for both economic and strategic purposes. He set about the restoration of devastated towns such Lismore, Tallow and Youghal, and planned four new towns for West Cork, namely Bandonbridge (Bandon), Clonakility, Enniskean and Castletown Kinneigh, which would serve as market towns for the planted areas and centres of defence against the Irish. Bandonbridge is one of the few 'new' towns of the Munster plantation for which there is a reasonably detailed account of its conception and original form. It was developed on a site near a ford on the Bandon river between Bantry and Cork, and early plans show a walled settlement with a grid-iron layout, with the sessions house and market place in the centre. A later plan reveals a larger town than that shown on the first, divided by the river into two parts, each fortified with walls and having within the grid-iron layout, a sessions house, market place and church, the two halves being linked by two bridges.[48] The houses were substantial, and each had a garden, so that they appeared to be standing in an orchard. In all, Boyle is estimated to have spent £14,000 on the town, which was given a grammar school and almshouses, and which was incorporated in 1613. Boyle's own description of the town in 1633 emphasises two of its three basic functions — as a strategic, Protestant, and industrial settlement:

> the circuit of my new town of Bandon is more in compass than that of Londonderry, that my walls are stronger, thicker and higher than theirs . . . In my towns there is built a strong bridge over the river,

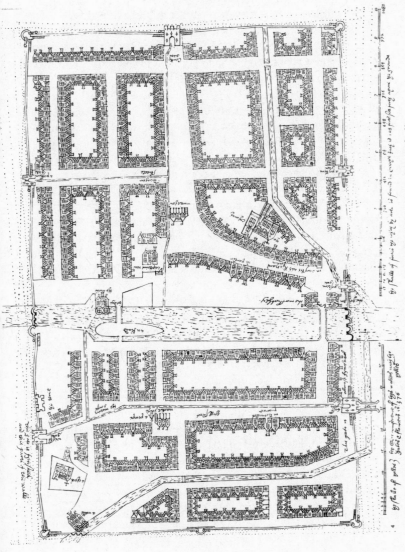

Figure 11: Bandonbridge, Co. Cork, c. 1615 (The town of Bandonbridge as it is now built, TCD. Ms 1209, no. 42)

two large sessions houses, two market houses, with two fair churches, which churches are so filled every Sabbath day with neat, orderly, religious peeple, as would comfort any good heart to see the change and behold such assemblies. No popish recusant or unconforming novellist being admitted to live in all the town.[49]

Bandon developed a prosperous linen industry, and this, together with her Protestantism, was deemed to have sustained the town, even in times of adversity. Bandon did not develop into a major regional centre, though it did survive, and was described in 1641 as ranking equal to towns like Drogheda and Kilkenny. Enniskean and Castletown Kinneigh, two other towns constructed by Boyle in West Cork, were not as strongly fortified as Bandonbridge, and were sacked during the 1641 rebellion. Clonakilty, which was incorporated in 1613, with a mayor (or 'sovereign') and a recorder, was planned by Boyle to become a seaport and major town in Cork. He built a large church there, and though its linen trade made it a kind of commercial centre, it never lived up to Boyle's hopes, though it survives today.

Boyle's attempts to construct new towns in Cork mark an important phase in Irish urban history, in that they indicated the practical import-ance of including towns as part of any plantation scheme: a doctrine which had been preached but hitherto rarely practised. Others had notions of similar schemes: Henry Coffe attempted in 1603 to interest members of the Dutch community in London in settling in West Cork, where he envisaged the building of two towns, at Crookhaven and Skull, as bases for settlement and for the exploitation of the rich fishing grounds off the coast.[50] His propaganda was apparently ineffective, as were many of the attempts to revive interest in the Munster plantation in the seventeenth century.

The Munster plantation was clearly not responsible for a wave of urbanisation in the south of Ireland, though the few successful develop-ments and some of the notional schemes for urban centres are of con-siderable interest. What is really significant, in a sense, is the moral drawn from the Munster plantation: that in future, attempts at civil colonisation must incorporate a higher density of nucleated settlement, including towns.

(iii) Ulster

The most far-reaching of the plantation schemes in Ireland was the plantation of Ulster, begun in 1609 and effectively terminated by the rebellion of 1641. It arose from the demise of Gaelic power in what had become, by the second half of the sixteenth century, the most trouble-some of the Irish provinces. The province was effectively isolated from the rest of the country by a range of physiographic barriers, including the drumlin belt (which stretches across the country from Dundalk to Sligo Bay on the west coast), the Erne river system and its many lakes in the west, the Mourne mountains, and the Slieve Gullion and Carling-ford mountains to the east. Much of the land was undrained bog and lake, with dense woods in many places, and the crossings and passes which could be used by the English forces to gain access to Ulster were frequently the scene of ambushes and skirmishes. Behind this physio-graphic frontier, the Gaelic way of life had been preserved, and succes-sive attempts to bring an Anglicised peace to the province had failed. The only English footholds in Ulster were the coastal towns founded by the Normans at Carrickfergus and Newry, and a network of military forts and garrisons which had been set up during the nine years' war (1594-1603) against the Ulster earls of Tyrconnell and Tyrone. The war had, in fact, ended in a negotiated peace, but the power of the Gaelic earls was substantially reduced, and Ulster experienced a process of Anglicisation of many facets of life, including administration, justice and land tenure. The diminution of the power of the old Gaelic order led to the 'flight' of the earls and a hundred of their followers to the Continent in August 1607. This departure presented an opportunity for the English government to complete the process of the Anglicisation of Ulster. The flight of the earls was deemed to be an admission of treason, their estates were declared forfeit to the Crown, and with great speed plans were made for a plantation of six of the counties of Ulster: Donegal, Coleraine, Tyrone, Armagh, Fermanagh and Cavan. The counties of Antrim and Down were not included, having been partly colonised by Gaelic-speaking Scots in the sixteenth century (notably those parts of Antrim known as 'The Route', and 'The Glens'), these having been allocated for colonisation organised by individual Scots and English undertakers. Even before the flight of the earls, James I had in 1605 given two-thirds of the large north Down estate of Con O'Neill to two Lowland Scots, Hugh Montgomery and James Hamilton, who were effective undertakers and colonisers. This transaction laid the foundation for extensive Scots colonisation of both Down and Antrim.

Various schemes for the plantation of the escheated counties of Ulster were put forward, but in 1609 articles for a plantation were drawn up in London, which provided for plantation by new settlers, soldiers and Irish. This scheme demonstrated a number of novel de-partures from previous plantations — provision was made, for example,

for the Irish to be given land, the City of London was 'encouraged' to
support the plantation by taking over the financing of the plantation in
the Coleraine (subsequently County Londonderry), and by the provisions made for urbanisation as part of the plantation process. The 1609
scheme made provision for 25 corporate towns to be built, which
would have rights for markets and fairs, various liberties, and members
of Parliament. Endowments of land were to be made to support urban
development, which would take the form of completely new towns on
new sites or the development of towns around pre-existing sites such as
military forts or native settlements.[51] However, like previous plantation
schemes, the implementation of plans drawn up in London was in
reality more difficult in Ireland. In this case, it was realised, even before
the plantation commissioner had left England (in 1610) that the plans
for the new towns were inadequate, and more detailed provisions were
made. Effectively, responsibility for design and layout was given to the
commissioner, and while the specifications are 'of interest from a
planning viewpoint, on this crucial question they represented not much
more than a facile transference of responsibility from London to
Dublin'.[52] Progress with the plantation was slow. In 1611, when further
revised views of the urban possibilities of the plantation had been put
forward, Lord Carew was sent to examine Irish affairs, including the
plantation, and revisions made to the plan of 1609. The 1609 plan had
provided for 25 new towns: this figure was reduced to sixteen, the less
realistic proposals, including those for towns at Innishowen, Dungiven,
in Loughinsolin barony, being abandoned, and some new sites being
substituted for those originally proposed. Fairly constant modifications
of the location, form and administrative bases of the new towns were a
consistent feature of the planned process of urbanisation, but the process did get under way, and by 1613 some fourteen of the new towns
had received charters of incorporation. This does not mean, of course,
that the towns had been completed: it is more a reflection of the
preparations for Parliament, 'involving as they did the creation of new
boroughs as a tactic to procure a pliable house of commons'.[53] Most
of the charters were issued to 'patrons' or 'superintendents' — plantation grantees who were required as a condition of their grant of land to
oversee the building of the town concerned within a limited period.
Derry and Coleraine, both in the Londoners' plantation, were re-incor-
porated within a short space of time, and their charters were more
elaborate than those of the other towns. By 1641, a total of sixteen
towns had been incorporated in the planted counties — nine less than
the numbers proposed in 1609, but equal to the revised number in the

1611 revision. Thus, in a relatively short space of time, a new urban network or system had been created and was the direct outcome of a political strategy. It has been suggested that the 1609 plan, particularly the provisions for new towns, was a good example of a 'regional' plan,[54] though with the *caveat* that the 'selection of town sites . . . was really considered as a county rather than on a regional basis'.[55] In practice, however, the end product was far from being a model of regional urban development, for a number of reasons. The distribution of the towns was, for example, very uneven — perhaps a reflection of strategic considerations which encouraged growth in areas of existing forts — but resulting in large areas which were not served by towns. This latter feature was emphasised by the reduction in the number of towns planned in 1609 — reflecting, perhaps, political and administrative difficulties and confusions and the lack of detailed geographical knowledge (though surveys of the escheated counties had been made).[56] Another 'failure' of the actual plantation was the failure to establish any number of reasonably sized and functionally effective urban centres. By 1641, the only sizeable plantation towns were Derry, Coleraine and Strabane, with many of the remaining 'towns' being little larger or functionally different from the villages of the planted areas. This marked lack of town growth was probably a result of the corporations being hampered by inadequate financial provision which, in some cases, resulted from the lack of initiative of the superintendence of the grantee. Thus: 'in leaving urban development — an important aspect of what may be called the institutional side of the plantation — to private initiative the planners incurred some responsibility for the subsequent slow and fitful growth of town life.'[57]

The new towns created by the plantation varied, therefore, in size, form and function. The two largest towns — Derry and Coleraine — were those financed by the City of London. Derry had been an ancient monastic settlement, and its site on the River Foyle had been regarded since the mid-sixteenth century as having strategic importance. In 1600 a small garrison was planted by Sir Henry Docwra. The new plantation town was an excellent example of a fortified planned town of Renaissance style: constructed with thick walls, bulwarks and a geometrical layout comprising a central square or 'diamond' into which ran the two main streets at right angles to each other. The market house, town hall and prison were located in a building in the town square. Pynnar's survey of 1618-19 describes Derry in the following terms:

The City of London-Derry is now compassed about with a very

Strong Wall, excellently made and neatly wrought; being all of good
Lime and Stone; the Circuit whereof is 283 perches and 2/3, at 18
feet to the Perch; besides the four gates which contain 84 feet; and
in every Place of the Wall it is 24 feet high, and six feet thick. The
gates are all battlemented, but to two of them there is no going up,
so that they serve no great use; neither have they made any Leaves
for their Gates; but make two Draw-Bridges serve for two of them,
and two Portcullises for the other two. The Bullwarks are very
large and good, being in number nine . . . Since the last survey there
is built a School, which is 67 feet in length and 25 in breadth, with
two other small Houses . . . The whole number of Houses within the
city is 92, and in them there are 102 Families, which are far too few
a number for the Defence of such a Circuit . . .[58]

By 1627, the number of houses had increased to 200. Coleraine had a
ground plan similar to that of Derry, though the defences were inferior.
Both towns were important marketing and distributing centres, with
extremely large hinterlands, and thus 'the inhabitants of both Derry
and Coleraine consisted, for the most part, of merchants, shop-keepers
and craftsmen'.[59]

The other towns of the planted counties were generally less impressive though they did have certain similarities of form – notably the
central square or 'diamond' and planned layouts – with the larger
towns. Apart from Derry, Coleraine and Strabane, the following towns
were incorporated: Dungannon, Clogher, Strabane, Augher, Limavady,
Lifford, Ballyshannon, Killybegs, Donegal, Enniskillen, Cavan,
Belturbet, Armagh and Charlemont. There were not all completely new
towns: Cavan and Armagh, for example, had long fulfilled urban functions prior to incorporation. The smaller towns were not walled, and
their corporate status was insufficient to protect them in 1641. They
usually had some kind of fort or fortified enclosure (bawn), the latter
normally associated with the manor house of the grantee. Because the
English settlers had little tradition of defensive building, the general
provisions for defence were inadequate: the bawns were not always
sufficiently strong, though some had corner-towers, and in some cases
were simply adaptations of native raths.[60] Apart from the stone houses
of the grantees, the other houses often took the form of 'cage' English
houses, built with black wooden frames and white plaster panels, and
without provisions for defence. The populations of the towns consisted
of soldiers, craftsmen, builders, merchants and shopkeepers. All these
characteristics are found in Pynnar's description of Lifford (in Donegal),

a new town built on the west bank of the Foyle; and of the town of Donegal:

> *Town of Lyffer.* A good and strong fort built of lime and stone, with bulwarks, a parapet, and a large ditch of good depth cast above it on the river side, with a storehouse for victuals and munition, a gate-house and a drawbridge . . . There is another small fort in the town rampiered and ditched, about which are certain houses built of good timber after the English manor, which serve for the use of a gaoler, and to keep prisoner. . . Upon view of the town we found it [1611] well furnished with inhabitants of English, and Scottish, and Irish, who live by several trades . . .
>
> *Town of Donegall.* We found a fair bawn built, with flankers, a para-pet, and a walk on the top 15 feet high. Within the bawn is a strong house of stone, built by Captain Basil Brooke. . . Many families of English, Scottish, and Irish are inhabiting in the town, who built them good copled houses after the manner of the Pale.[61]

There were, of course, new towns being created outside the escheated counties. This is particularly true of the areas colonised in Antrim and Down. Newtownards was erected on the Ards peninsula by Sir Hugh Montgomery, and Bangor, Holywood and Killyleagh were built by Sir James Hamilton in north Down, all on the land confiscated from Con O'Neill. The most important of the new towns was Belfast. Prior to the seventeenth century, there had been little to mark the site of the future city except a small castle guarding a ford on the Lagan, which was rebuilt by Sir Arthur Chichester. Chichester acquired a grant of the castle and surrounding lands in 1603 and began the building of a town around the castle. A description of 1611 states that: 'The Towne of Bealfast is plotted out in good forme, wherein are many fameleys of English, Scotch, and some Manksmen already inhabitinge, of which some are artificers who have buylte good tymber houses with chimneys. . .'[62] Quays were built, markets established, and a fair was in existence from 1604. A charter of incorporation was granted in 1613 (mainly to increase Protestant representation in Parliament), and by 1641 commercial activity, and some industries including the brewing of ale, leather-tanning, and iron-smelting, were flourishing. It was in the second half of the century, however, that the growth of Belfast really began.

An effective hiatus in the story of urban development in Ulster occurs in 1641, when the Ulster Irish rose against the English, and the

vulnerability of many of the new settlements to attack was clearly
demonstrated. Nevertheless, the Ulster plantations had laid the urban
foundations of Ulster, and left an inheritance which in every way is
manifestly obvious even to the present day.

(iv) Other Plantations

Efforts were made to put the Irish plantations' experience to good use
in a number of other plantation schemes in the reign of James I. There
were minor schemes of plantation in predominantly Irish areas: in parts
of Wexford, Longford, Leitrim and Offaly, though they were largely
unsuccessful in the aim of establishing a strong Protestant population.
In the Leitrim plantation, the 'new' towns of Jamestown and
Carrick-on-Shanon were established, but the contribution of these
plantations to urban development in Ireland was negligible.

(v) The Older Towns in the Period 1540-1641

The period 1540-1641 was one of mixed fortunes for the older towns
of Ireland. The larger port towns continued to enjoy prosperity, albeit
to varying degrees, largely due to their external trading links, and maintained their autonomy. This latter feature was important to the
Elizabethan and Stuart efforts to pacify Ireland, for throughout the
rebellions in Munster and elsewhere, the port towns maintained their
loyalty and thus acted as strong points for defence and as bases for
offensive military action against the rebels. Such towns were, of course,
frequently subject to attack, which left some of them in rather dilapi-
dated condition. Two other factors operated during this period to
counteract the prosperous development of Irish towns, notably those
of the south. These were the effect of the growing intensity of English
dislike of Irish trade with France and Spain, and the decline, in the
early seventeenth century, of the herring shoals off the south coast.

Dublin remained the largest and most important city: described by
Moryson as:

> the Chief City of the Kingdom, and seat of justice fairly built, fre-
> quently inhabited, and adorned with a strong Castle, fifteen
> churches, an Episcopal seat, and a fair College, — an happy founda-
> tion of an university laid in our age, — and endowed with many
> privileges.[63]

Trinity College, the first (and only) college of the University of Dublin,
founded in 1591 by charter from Elizabeth, was the first university to

be founded in Ireland — and the only one until the nineteenth century — an indication of the relative cultural poverty of the Irish towns compared with their Scots, English and Continental European counterparts. The existence of the bar at the approach to Dublin was a partial deterrent to her maritime trade, but the size and quality of demand for imported goods of very high quality — generated by the presence of governor, council and a host of administrators and officials — was perhaps sufficient incentive for merchants to put their vessels at risk by sending them to Dublin. By the beginning of the seventeenth century there are signs that Dublin was beginning to expand, with the

> cage-work houses of the Tudor period . . . giving way to buildings of stone and brick. In appearance and character it was the most English city in Ireland; its economic and political importance depended almost wholly on the English connection, and its trade was mainly with London, whose fashion the nobility and leading citizens were always eager to follow.[64]

The seventeenth century, particularly after the Restoration, was to be a time of unprecedented expansion for Dublin. It must not be forgotten, however, that at the end of the Elizabethan era it still had some of the characteristics of a 'colonial' town, for raids by the Irish from the Wicklow mountains on the suburbs of the city were frequent and devastating. The generally violent nature of life is illustrated by reference to several events of the last quarter of the sixteenth century: the city was ravaged by plague in 1575; in 1586 the Exchequer, by the east gate of the city, was plundered by Irish from the Wicklow mountains; in 1596, '144 barrels of powder, intended for Dublin Castle, blew up at Wood Quay, destroyed forty to fifty houses, and killed upwards of three hundred persons, and damaged several churches'.[65]

By 1600 Galway had become strongly fortified, because of the disorderly state of Connaught and the fear of a Spanish invasion. The city had probably reached its zenith at about this time, and a progressive decline set in during the seventeenth century, generally because of the unproductive hinterland which surrounded it, the discouragement of trade with Spain, and its remoteness from England. The main ports of Munster were Cork, Limerick and Waterford. There is evidence that some steps had been taken to expand Cork by the reclamation of marshland to the north-east by about 1600. The city, like Limerick, had suffered from the devastations of the Desmond rebellions and wars

in Munster, but Cork recovered quite quickly, while Limerick did not.
By the 1620s, in fact, the fine fortifications and houses of Limerick
were seen by commentators as indicative of former rather than contemporary prosperity.[66] Waterford remained an important and prosperous port town, with its 'commodious haven' seen, by Moryson, as
'a rich and well-inhabited city, esteemed the second to Dublin'.[67] The
most important of the smaller ports of Ireland were, at the beginning
of the seventeenth century, Wexford, Youghal, Drogheda and Dundalk.
Wexford suffered increasing decline in the early decades of the seventeenth century as a consequence of the migration of the herring shoals,
and Youghal had been subject to much devastation during the wars in
Munster, though it had experienced some increased prosperity during
the Munster plantation. The military activities in the north of Ireland
in late Elizabethan and early Stuart times had re-orientated the direction of some of the trade with Britain, and ports like Drogheda and
Dundalk had benefitted accordingly. Of the inland towns, few escaped
the assaults of rebel and military action, and towns like Armagh,
Kilmallock and Athenry were severely affected, some of them never
recovering their former prosperity and status.

Urban Development c. 1641-1700

At the beginning of the seventeenth century, the Irish urban system
and its individual components still bore the hallmarks of a medieval
system. Peripherally located — on the coast for the most part — the
towns were mainly walled, small in area and relatively static in terms
of growth. By the end of the century the situation had changed completely, notably in respect of the rise of the new towns of Ulster and
the spectacular increase in the size and significance of Dublin.

The reasons for this quite dramatic change are not too hard to
identify. They include population increase, changes in rural production
and patterns and volume of trade (notably exports) and, inevitably,
political and military activities and policies. Urban development in
Ireland in the seventeenth century was not characterised by constant
progress — vide the fate of some of the new towns of Ulster, and indeed
of some of the older towns which supported the Catholic confederacy.
Temporary arrest of progress, and in some cases the beginnings of
decline, were also brought about by Cromwellian military activity, by
plague, and by the eclipsing of some of the smaller port towns by their
growing neighbours.

A measure of urban growth in the seventeenth century is provided
by the change in their populations. No accurate quasi-census material

exists, and only crude approximations can be made, based on contemporary estimates, the relative size of towns as they appeared on maps, and the Hearth Tax returns. Estimates for the population of Ireland as a whole suggest that the population of the country doubled during the century, from about 1.4 million to 2.8 million people,[68] with a slight decline taking place in the 1650s and 1660s, largely caused by plague, and an accelerated increase in the last three decades of the century. Earlier estimates had put the Irish population at the beginning of the century at about half a million, but this would seem to be far too low, for this figure would require a four-fold increase in population between 1600 and 1700, for which there is no clear evidence. The population of the major towns in 1600 have been estimated by Cullen as Dublin 5,000, Galway less than 4,200, Limerick c. 2,400–3,600, and Waterford and Cork c. 2,400 each,[69] indicating that only Dublin's population had reached 60,000 by 1680,[70] exceeding 70,000 by the end of the century. That of Cork was about 20,000 by c. 1680, and Waterford and Galway had 5,000 to 6,000 each. These large increases in population reflect, *inter alia*, the large expansion in trade of the major port cities, the increasing polarisation of urban development, and the achievement of primate city status by Dublin. They also indicate a change in the urban hierarchy, marked particularly by the rise of Cork and by the relative demise of Galway. The pace of change of urban population appears to have varied throughout the century. The population of Dublin appears to have increased steadily from 1600 to 1660, to about 25,000 to 30,000, then almost doubled in the next twenty years, and then increased more slowly to the end of the century. The expansion of Cork was also steady until mid-century, when it expanded rapidly to the end of the century. Galway, in contrast, expanded in the first half of the century, but then declined. Limerick and Waterford appear to have had a steady rate of expansion through the century.

It appears that one of the principal causes of these relative changes in status and size of Irish towns was change in the pattern and volume of trade. The 'final' conquest of Ireland produced a closer orientation of trade to England, and at the same time the opportunities opened up by the new political stability for profitable enterprise, both in rural and urban areas, encouraged a renewed flow of immigrants. The gradual disappearance of the pirates from the Irish coastal waters, and the disaffection with Continental countries, notably Spain, enhanced the increased importance of the Irish trade with England. As a consequence there was a marked rise in Irish exports to England in the 1620s and 1630s, and, after a setback in the 1640s and 1650s, the momentum continued. By the 1660s three-quarters of Irish exports went to England. In the earlier part of the century it was in the export of Irish wool that the greatest increase was experienced. This was due to the suitability of Irish wool to the 'new draperies' of England and elsewhere. Later in the century it was the export of live cattle, stimulated by the demands of the London food market, which assumed dominance, though this was changed by the various cattle acts of 1663 and 1666. The ports which benefited most from this general increase in trade were Dublin and Cork, whose range of exports was sufficiently varied to safeguard them against decline resulting from decrease in exports of any single commodity. In the period 1664-9, 40 per cent of the Irish customs revenue was provided by Dublin, which had a vast hinterland which included the principal wool-producing areas, and which expanded so effectively that by the last twenty years of the century it had eroded part of the hinterland of Galway, to which land access had always been difficult.

The general momentum in the Irish economy was temporarily halted in the period of the 1640s and 1650s. The rising in Ulster in 1641, and the activities of the Catholic confederacy, together with the consequences of Cromwell's devastating reaction, ushered in a period of plague, famine, depression and population decline. During the 1640s, many of the towns, because of the influence of the Catholic 'Old English' resident in them, had supported or harboured the confederates. They also had large Irish populations. Cromwellian legislation excluded Catholics from residence or office-holding in the towns, and the 'clearing' of the Irish from some towns left them virtually in ruins. Galway, for example, which was the last of the Irish towns to surrender to the Cromwellian forces (in 1652), suffered heavy taxation and deprivation, as Waterford, Limerick, Cork and Kilkenny also experienced 'clearance' of the Irish and decay. Two places which largely escaped such acts were Belfast and Dublin. The general effect of the Cromwellian policies for a conquered Ireland was to secure, in both rural areas and towns, the ascendancy and interests of the Protestant population, which had gradually been expanding since the late sixteenth century. This fact, plus the various efforts of the parliamentary government to restore the Irish economy to a more healthy state, including the setting up of a council of trade, paved the way for the spectacular phase of urban growth which followed the Restoration, of which the most dramatic example is Dublin.

The arrival of the new Lord Lieutenant of Ireland, the Duke of Ormonde, in Dublin in July 1662, marked the beginnings of an important phase of urban development for the capital city. Dublin at this point was not an attractive city, with many of its buildings, including the castle and Christ Church Cathedral, in very poor condition, but during the twenty-five years of the reign of Charles II it expanded rapidly. One of the first and most grandiose schemes for the improvement of Dublin was, in fact, the formation of Phoenix Park, largely at Ormonde's initiative. The purpose of this undertaking 'was to create a royal deer-park (and therefore in practice a public park), rather than a mere demesne surrounding the vice-regal residence'[71] (the latter having been built in 1618 on land to the northwest of the city). Some 2,000 acres of land were acquired, and deer, partridges and pheasants purchased, and though part of the area was subsequently allocated to the Royal Hospital at Kilmainham, founded in 1680, Phoenix Park remains a distinctive part of Dublin today. Other notable developments included the layout of St Stephen's Green, a 27-acre green surrounded by 89 house-plots, which were allocated by ballot to the wealthier citizens of the city, and the development, as another suburb, of the old green at Oxmantown, north-west of the city. Much of the new building was outside the limits of the old city, and it has been estimated that 'by the end of Charles II's reign more of the city was outside the walls than inside them'.[72] Most of the development prior to 1673 was to the south and east of the city, and included the new Trinity College and Dame Street, St Stephen's Green, and the development on the Aungier estate. In fact the 'first extensive planned suburban development in Dublin took place from 1660 to 1685 on the estate owned and administered by Francis Aungier, the first earl of Longford',[73] which was located to the south of the castle and west of St Stephen's Green. There was little development west and north of the city, apart from the King's Inns on the quay on the north side. From 1673 to 1685 there was surburban development on the north side of the river, following the reclamation of a creek and the building of three new quays on the north bank. Access to the new northern suburbs was improved by the building of three bridges — making four in all — in the period 1673-85, though the bridges were obstacles to boats on the Liffey.

Contemporary descriptions of the city emphasise its appearance and its status. A note in the 1695 edition of Camden's *Brittania* states that 'Dublin is more than as big again as when Camden wrote, the buildings more sumptuous and the city every way more pleasant and wholesome,'[74] and Boate's *Natural History of Ireland*, originally produced in 1652, speaks of Dublin as 'the chief city of the whole commonwealth, the residence of the governer, the Council of State, all the great officers, the exchequers, judges, and courts of justice'.[75] The importance of trade to Dublin is also stressed:

> It is situated in the province of Leinster, about the middle of the length of Ireland, not far from the sea, an inlet whereof maketh a harbour for this city; which harbour, although none of the best in Ireland . . . is nevertheless frequented with more ships, and hath greater importation of all things, than any other haven in the kingdom; by reason that all sorts of commodities are much more readily and in greater plenty vented here than anywhere else, what in the city itself, being great and populous, what into the country, for in the time of peace almost all Leinster and Ulster were wont to furnish themselves from Dublin of all kinds of provisions and necessaries, such as were brought in out of foreign countries.[76]

Dublin was the most important of the Irish ports, most of her trade being with England. The main exports were wool and friezes, and the principal imports included coal, drapery, hops, tobacco, timber, wine and salt.

The considerable increase in population which Dublin experienced in the period 1660-85 was in large measure due to immigration, with the major immigration from outside Ireland coming from England. It was estimated that in the period 1672-87 35,000 English immigrants came to Ireland, many of them to Dublin,[77] and there was also significant immigration of French, Dutch and Germans, mainly merchants and craftsmen. During the period 1671-82 there was a very large increase in the Catholic population of Dublin.

The social geography of Dublin at this time can be tentatively reconstructed on the basis of the Hearth Tax returns,[78] and the evidence suggests a high concentration, at mid-century, of the wealthier and more important people in certain parts of the older, central parishes of the medieval city within the city walls, with the poorer sections of the populace having a more peripheral location, many of them living outside the walls. With the considerable expansion of the city in the last quarter of the century, however, there is evidence of movement by the wealthier class outwards, to the new suburbs (like St Stephen's Green and Oxmantown), and an increasing concentration of the poorer people in the city centre, a movement which accelerated in the eighteenth century and produced squalid conditions in the centre of the city. Such a development in the late seventeenth century may be seen, in Vance's terms, as indicative of Dublin's progress from a 'medieval' to a 'capitalist' city.[79]

Dublin's primacy in the Irish urban hierarchy can clearly be measured by its population size, range of functions, and trading activities, to which no other Irish town approximated. That is not to say, however, that town life did not flourish elsewhere in Ireland. Cork had experienced rapid growth, and had risen to become the second-largest city. It was described by Sir Richard Cox in 1687 as

> the second best city of Ireland . . . generally inhabited by English and those industrious and rich; it is a happy situation for trade by land or sea, for it is a great thoroughfare and has an incomparable harbour. The suburbs are grown twice as big as the city, and altogether do contain 20,000 souls.[80]

The prosperity of Cork, like that of Dublin, derived mainly from trade, in this case the provisions trade (mainly salted beef) to the colonies and plantations in North America, and had eclipsed that of Waterford. Galway had entered a period of relative decline, though it participated for a time in the increasing trade with the West Indies. The rising urban star on the horizon was Belfast, which reached a population of about 2,000 by the end of the century. Belfast had not been greatly affected by the troublesome period of the forties and fifties, and developed a major export trade based on the Irish rural economy — cattle products and corn being major export items. The period from 1660 onward was a period of notable expansion in trade, mainly with England, Scotland, North America and Europe. Imports included linen, wine, brandy, fruit, spices, timber and tobacco. In 1666, sugar-refining was begun. The main period of expansion of this city, however, like that of other towns in Ulster, had yet to come.

The most significant factors conditioning urban development in the second half of the seventeenth century were the fluctuating political relations between England and Ireland, as expressed in rebellions, confederation and extreme military action, and the reorientation of trade consequent on the new peace of the late- and post-Commonwealth period and of the rise of the North American colonies. The policy of developing new plantation-style towns was largely abandoned, and the few 'new' towns, like St Johnstown in Longford, that were built did not achieve real urban size or functions. By 1700, therefore, the main elements of the urban system of Ireland had been established, and it is quite a remarkable and perhaps unique feature, in western European experience, that there has been little addition of towns to that system to the present day.

Notes

1. K.S. Bottigheimer, *English Money and Irish Land. The 'Adventurers' in the Cromwellian Settlement of Ireland* (Oxford, 1971), p. 5.
2. G. Sjoberg, 'The Rise and Fall of Cities; a Theoretical Perspective', *International Jnl. of Comparative Sociology*, I (1963), pp. 107-8.
3. Ibid., p. 114.
4. Ibid., p. 112.
5. Bottigheimer, *English Money and Irish Land*, p. 5.
6. W.F.T. Butler, 'Town Life in Medieval Ireland', *J. Cork Hist. and Arch. Soc.,* VIII, 2nd ser. (1901), p. 17.
7. J. Hicks, *A Theory of Economic History* (Oxford, 1969).
8. Ibid., p. 38.
9. Ibid., p. 39.
10. A.K. Longfield, *Anglo-Irish Trade in the Sixteenth Century* (London, 1929).
11. K. Nicholls, *Gaelic and Gaelicised Ireland in the Middle Ages* (Dublin, 1972), p. 121.
12. W. Camden, *Britannia*, E. Gibson (ed.) (London, 1695), p. 979.
13. *Calendar of State Papers. Ireland. 1601-03. Addenda. 1565-1654*, (London, 1912), p. 4.
14. Richard Stanihurst, *A treatise containing a plain and perfect description of Ireland*, vi (London, 1808), p. 21.
15. *Calendar of State Papers. Ireland. 1601-3*, p. 662.
16. Ibid.
17. A.R. Orme, 'Youghal, county Cork – growth, decay, resurgence', *Ir. Geogr.,* V, No. 3 (1966), p. 129 seq.
18. Stanihurst, *A treatise . . .,* p. 21.
19. Camden, *Britannia*, p. 994.
20. Stanihurst, *A treatise . . .,* p. 21.
21. Ibid., p. 157.
22. R. Stewig, *Dublin, Funktionen und Entwicklung* (Kiel, 1959), p. 63.
23. Longfield, 'Anglo-Irish Trade in the Sixteenth Century', *Proc. Roy. Irish Acad.,* XXVI, C, No. 17 (1924), p. 323 *seq*.
24. M.D. O'Sullivan, 'The Fortification of Galway in the Sixteenth and Seventeenth Centuries', *J. Galway Arch. and Hist. Soc.,* XVI (1924), p. 2.
25. Camden, *Britannia*, p. 1002.
26. Edmund Campion, *Two Bokes of the Histories of Ireland* (1571), A.F. Vossen (ed) (Assen, 1963), p. [8].
27. O'Sullivan, *J. Galway Arch. and Hist. Soc.,* XVI (1934), p.7-24.
28. J. Hardiman, *History of the town and county of Galway* (Dublin, 1820; reprinted Galway, 1958), p. 83.
29. Stanihurst, *A treatise . . .,* p. 30.
30. T.W. Freeman, *Ireland* (London, 4th edn., 1969), p. 387.
31. Nicholls, *Gaelic and Gaelicised Ireland*, p. 122.
32. See D.A. Gillmor, 'The Development of Sligo as a Regional Capital', *Geographical Vewpoint* (Dublin), 4 (1967), pp. 191-200.
33. J. Otway-Ruthven, *Liber Primus Kilkenniensis* (Kilkenny, 1961).
34. Ibid., p. 119.
35. Ibid., p. 110.
36. Ibid., p. 103.

37. Ibid., p. 96.

38. Nicholls, *Gaelic and Gaelicised Ireland*, p. 122.

39. Statute Rolls of the Parliament of Ireland, 1st to 12th years Edward IV, p. 139: cited by Art Cosgrave, 'The Gaelic Resurgence and the Geraldine Supremacy', in T.W. Moody and F.X. Martin (eds.), *The Course of Irish History* (Cork, 1967), p. 164.

40. 'A Chorographic Account of the Southern Part of the County of Wexford, Written Anno 1684 . . ', H.F. Hore (ed.), *Jnl. Kilkenny and S.E. Ireland Arch. Soc.*, II, n.s. (1858-9), p. 455.

41. G.A. Hayes-McCoy, 'The Tudor Conquest', in Moody and Martin (eds.), *The Course of Irish History*, p. 176.

42. Ibid., p. 178.

43. J.H. Andrews, 'Geography and Government in Elizabethan Ireland', in N. Stephens and R.E. Glasscock (eds.), *Irish Geographical Studies* (Belfast, 1970), p. 182.

44. D.B. Quinn, 'The Munster Plantation: problems and opportunities', *J. Cork Hist. and Arch.Soc.*, 71 (1966), p. 22.

45. Andrews, *Irish Geographical Studies*, p. 186.

46. Quinn, *J. Cork. Hist and Arch.Soc.*, 71 (1966), p. 24.

47. G.A. Hayes-McCoy, 'The Completion of the Tudor Conquest and the advance of the Counter-Reformation, 1571-1603' in T.W. Moody, F.X. Martin and F.J. Byrne (eds.), *A New History of Ireland*, vol. III (Oxford, 1976).

48. R.A. Butlin, 'Urban Genesis in Ireland, 1556-1641', in R.W. Steel and R. Lawton (eds.), *Liverpool Essays in Geography* (London, 1967), pp. 218-19.

49. D. Townshend, *The Life and letters of the Great Earl of Cork* (London, 1904), p. 44.

50. Quinn, *J. Cork Hist. and Arch.Soc.*, 71 (1966), p. 35.

51. R.J. Hunter, 'Towns in the Ulster plantation', *Studia Hibernica*, 11 (1972); G. Camblin, *The Town in Ulster*, (Belfast, 1951).

52. Hunter, *Studia Hibernica*, 11 (1972), p. 11.

53. Ibid., p. 57.

54. Camblin, *The Town in Ulster*, p. 17.

55. Ibid., p. 21.

56. J.H. Andrews, 'The Maps of the Escheated Counties of Ulster, 1609-10', *Proc.Roy.Irish Acad.*, 74, Section C, No. 4 (1974), pp. 133-70.

57. Hunter, *Studia Hibernica*, 11 (1972), p. 55.

58. G. Hill, *An Historical Account of the Plantation of Ulster at the Commencement of the Seventeenth century* (Belfast, 1877; reprinted Shannon, 1970), p. 574.

59. Camblin, *The Town of Ulster*, p. 33.

60. E.M. Jope, 'Moyry, Charlemont, Castleraw, and Richhill: fortification to architecture in the North of Ireland 1570-1700', *Ulster Journal of Archaeology*, 3rd series, 23 (1960), p. 112.

61. Hill, *Plantation of Ulster*, p. 514.

62. 1611 survey, cited in J.C. Beckett and R.E. Glasscock (eds.), *Belfast – Origin and Growth of an Industrial City* (London, 1967), p. 24.

63. Fynes Moryson, 'Description of Ireland', in R.L. Falkiner, *Illustrations of Irish History and Topography* (London, 1904), p. 416.

64. J.C. Beckett, *The Making of Modern Ireland 1603-1923* (London, 1966), p. 30.

65. A. Marmion, *The Ancient and Modern History of the Maritime Ports of Ireland* (London, 1860), pp. 213-14.

66. Beckett, *The Making of Modern Ireland*, p. 31.

67. Moryson, *Description of Ireland*, p. 415.
68. L.M. Cullen, 'Economic Trends, 1660-91', in Moody, Martin and Byrne (eds.), *A New History of Ireland*, Vol. III (Oxford, 1976).
69. Ibid., p. 6.
70. R.A. Butlin, 'The population of Dublin in the late seventeenth century', *Ir. Geogr.*, V, 2 (1965), pp. 51-66.
71. M. Craig, *Dublin 1660-1860* (Dublin, 1969), p. 15.
72. J.G. Simms, 'Dublin in 1685', *Irish Historical Studies*, XIV, 55 (1965), p. 21
73. N.T. Burke, 'An early modern Dublin suburbs: the estate of Francis Aungier, Earl of Longford', *Irish Geography* VI, 4 (1972), p. 372.
74. Camden, *Brittania* (1695 edn.), p. 994.
75. Gerard Boate, *Ireland's Natural History* (London, 1755 edn.), pp. 5-6.
76. Ibid.
77. Simms, *Irish Hist. Studies*, XIV, 55 (1965), p. 216.
78. Butlin, *Ir. Geogr.*, V (1965), pp. 58-66.
79. S.W. Vance, 'Land assignment in the Precapitalist, Capitalist and Post Capitalist City', *Econ. Geogr.*, 47 (1971), pp. 101-20; see also John Langton, 'Residential patterns in pre-industrial cities: some case studies from seventeenth-century Britain', *Transactions, Institute of British Geographers*, 65 (1975), pp. 1-28; and J.H. Andrews, 'Land and People, c. 1685', being Chapter XVIII of T.W. Moody, F.X. Martin and F.J. Byrne (eds.), *A New History of Ireland*, III, *Early Modern Ireland* (1976), pp. 476-7
80. Sir Richard Cox, 'Regnum Corcagiense; or A Description of the Kingdom of Cork' (1687), in *Jnl. Cork Hist. and Arch.Soc.*, 2nd series, VIII, 54 (1902), p. 160.

4 IRISH TOWNS IN THE EIGHTEENTH AND NINETEENTH CENTURIES

T.W. Freeman

'Here are handsome quays where the smaller ships lie and load. This is a large and populous city, having many merchants in it. It is encompassed by a good wall of stone, but not many guns', wrote Francis Rogers[1] of Cork in a book of 1703. He adds that its merchants dealt with Bristol men who went to islands of the West Indies with beef, pork, butter, candles and other goods and that there was a very large retail market. The people of Cork, then as now, were 'generally given to hospitality, civil and courteous to strangers'. They were also 'refined', for they followed 'pretty much the French air in conversation, bringing up their children to dance, play on the fiddle, and fence, if they can give them nothing else'. Possibly the population at the beginning of the eighteenth century had reached 25,000, for the town had already spread beyond its walled enclosure on islands in the river to the neighbouring hillsides with their delightful views of the river Lee flowing out to the ramifying channels of Cork harbour. Not all the travellers to Cork wrote as favourably as William Rogers, for many found the contrast between a small number of rich merchants and a large number of poor workless people in overcrowded slums a sad spectacle; and some of them went further, for they thought the wealthy should care more for developing industry and trade and less for the pursuit of sport, entertainment and a life of elegance or even ostentation. That there were such contrasts in other Irish towns, probably in all, has been made abundantly clear over and over again, and notably so by C.E. Maxwell in her books on Dublin and on the entire country in the Georgian period.[2] Charity was favoured as a beneficial activity both to the donor and the recipient without questioning why it should be so universally necessary. Elegance in public buildings, as well as in the homes of those with adequate means, was sought and main streets were laid out handsomely with buildings of Wicklow granite or brick in Dublin, and of stone or brick in some places covered with stucco, elsewhere. The hospitals, government buildings, churches and other premises included some examples of the work of distinguished architects from England as well as of Irishmen and from 1757 the Wide Streets Commissioners were able to make, in Dublin, Cork, Limerick and elsewhere, those

handsome streets which, however altered by later building, are still fine
features of Irish towns.[3] In many places the example of the greater
cities was copied for a large number of towns, and even smaller places
that would now be regarded as villages were rebuilt by the local land-
owners during the eighteenth century, using the stately planning
fashions of the time which included the interplay of straight and
curved streets, of crescents and squares around parks and the careful
placing of monuments or buildings to provide a vista, terminating
perhaps in the classically columned entrance of a church with a fine
spire. The Georgian planner knew how to build a gracious town for the
rich, a small minority in the population. Fortunately virtually all the
travellers of the day and a certain proportion of the residents were
sufficiently observant to discern — in a general but in a few cases a
more specific way — what lay beyond the elegant life of the squares,
crescents and town streets.

How many people lived in towns at the beginning of the eighteenth
century is not known. It can only have been a small proportion of the
total population of Ireland, which has been estimated at approximately
2,000,000 in 1700. MacLysaght quotes an estimate[4] of 60,224 for
Dublin in 1706, 'probably rather less than the correct figure', with
25,000 in Cork, 11,000 in Limerick, 6,000 in Waterford and 6,000 in
Galway. All these, it will be noted, are ports but Kilkenny, with 7,000
people, was regarded as a major inland town. Belfast[5] was quite a small
place, recorded as having 2,000 inhabitants in 1685, and Derry had
almost 3,000 by 1700. The whole pattern of towns in Ireland was based
on the need for markets, normally held at least once a week, and on
fairs held at less frequent intervals.[6] Many towns had Anglo-Norman,
Tudor or Stuart town charters with a patent for holding fairs and
markets. Some of the places to which charters were given remained
small, yet their possession of trading facilities for the rural community
gave them the first and most essential function of any town in any age.
That all the major centres in 1700, except for Kilkenny, were ports was
indicative of the dependence of Ireland on maritime trade, and it is no
accident that in the Norse period Dublin, Wexford, Waterford, Cork
and Limerick were chosen by the invaders as major trading posts.
Inevitably towns were associated with government for in them justice
was dispensed and control exercised, in many cases by military force.
To this day nothing is more suggestive of fear of rebellion than the
barracks of Athlone on the west side of the Shannon, the traditional
divide between the provinces of Leinster and Connacht. And in the
towns of Ulster, mostly founded in the Stuart period, protection from

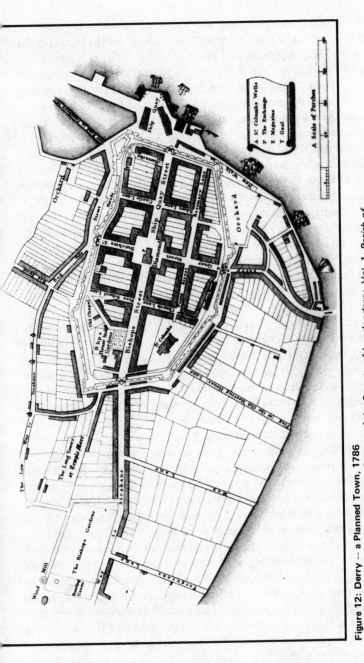

Figure 12: Derry — a Planned Town, 1786
This map was published in *Ordnance Survey of the County of Londonderry*, Vol. 1, *Parish of Templemore* (Dublin, 1837). Fundamentally it was a plantation town, designed for defence but with fine streets, a great church, and dignified houses. From the Diamond there is a street descending to the quay beside the Foyle and the growth of the town beyond the walls will be seen.

enemies was linked with the development of commerce: no town showed this better than Derry, with its walls, its central Market in the Diamond, its court house and prison as well as its finely placed cathedral of the Established Church (Figure 12). Sjoberg has written splendidly of the 'pre-industrial' town[7] and his work is valued for its emphasis on the concepts possessed by planners for the greater part of historical times: the town was an expression of a society's power and culture as well as of its commerce and craftsmanship. That some Irish towns preserved different quarters for its inhabitants, such as Carrickfergus with its English, Scotch and Irish towns, was indicative of the importation of the town as an alien institution to Ireland, but in fact the Irish penetrated the towns so effectively that by the eighteenth century such distinctions meant little in places such as Galway where the (somewhat eccentric) English traveller John Dunton[8] noted in 1699 that 'the inhabitants are generally Irish papists' with few Protestants except 'the soldiery quartered there which commonly are one regiment'. But though Protestants were few their great church of St Nicholas dominated the town and already had its famous peal of bells, 'a great rarity in all the country churches here'.

Although industry was not prominent in the towns, they normally had a flour mill, probably also a brewery and a distillery (or more than one), and in some places also woollen mills by the eighteenth century. And the numerous ports, many now almost forgotten, had extensive warehouses, so large in some places that it seemed that they could never at any time be filled, and in fact never were, as W.M. Thackeray and other nineteenth-century travellers commented.[9] Through the eighteenth century there was some home production of linen, mostly sold in the local markets but by the nineteenth century this had become almost completely restricted to the north-east, where it became the basis of a flourishing textile industry. Both domestic spinning and weaving survived into the mid-nineteenth century in Ulster although the returns for labour were very small, even negligible. The Industrial Revolution came to Ireland only in the nineteenth century, and then only in any strength to the north-east through the growth of the textile industry and shipbuilding, with associated engineering and other trades. By 1851, Great Britain had more than half its population in towns and the Census Commissioners were obviously impressed by the staggering growth of the mining and industrial towns.[10] Probably the town population was underestimated, for many places were under rural administration, though in fact they had become towns in size and functions. Comparisons with Irish towns of that date have little meaning, as in

1851 there was still a substantial number of people in hospitals and other institutions but in 1841 only 20 per cent of the population (then 8,175,000) lived in any form of clustered settlement (defined in the Census as having 20 houses or more) and less than 15 per cent in places having 1,500 people or more (Figure 13).[11] These figures indicate an economic complexion in which industry was of quite minor significance. Even by 1891, little over one-quarter of the Irish population (1,202,000 out of 4,705,000) lived in towns of more than 1,500 people. This classification is not entirely satisfactory for without doubt many much smaller places were towns in function: the 1841 Census Commissioners however, show something of the social concern of their time, for they define 'civic districts' as those having 2,000 or more people.[12] They included the population of

all towns contained less than that number as RURAL. This number may seem too low. But on the whole we considered it the best limit, as in Ireland although a town of 2,000 inhabitants seldom possesses any manufacture or trade of sufficient consequence or any division of occupation sufficiently distinct, to give it the principal characteristics of a town; yet we found, that when that number was accumulated, the evils of crowded habitations, which constitute another characteristic of a town, began to be felt, especially in a sanatory [*sic.*] point of view.

Obviously the Commissioners were fully aware of the growing problems presented by town growth in Britain, where the agitation for public health measures was widespread, and chose a parameter to solve their problem, or to attempt to do so, much as quantitative geographers do in modern times. But they did not succeed, nor did they claim to succeed, in defining a town as distinct from a village.

Roads in the early eighteenth century were maintained by the landlords and their tenants and in general were of reasonable quality, though in some areas they were poor and in the remoter parts of the west non-existent. One comment of Arthur Young is often quoted:[13]

For a country so far behind us as Ireland, to have got suddenly so much the start of us in the article of roads, is a spectacle that cannot fail to strike the English traveller exceedingly . . . I will go here; I will go there: I could trace a route upon paper as wild as fancy could dictate, and everywhere I found beautiful roads without break or hindrance to enable me to realize my design . . . in England . . . the

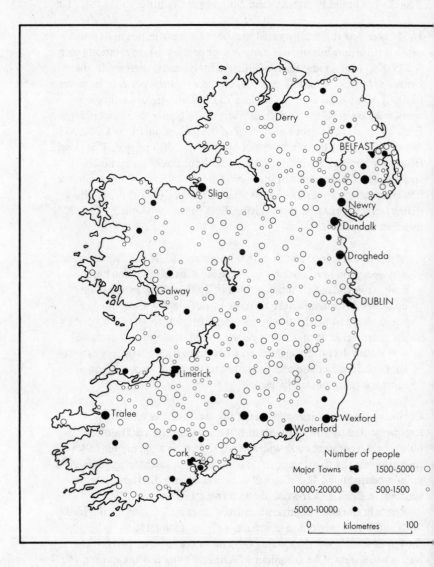

Figure 13: Towns in 1841
Only five towns, Dublin, Belfast, Cork, Limerick and Waterford had more than 20,000 people and over most of Ireland there was a network of towns and market villages of which some were too small to appear on this map. On the Atlantic coast Limerick, Galway and Sligo were major centres but in west Kerry, the west of Connaught and west Donegal there were few places that were recognisable as towns. Based on the map first published in *Pre-Famine Ireland* (Manchester, 1957), p. 26.

roads are about in as bad a state as in the time of Philip and Mary.

He goes on to describe the presentment road-building system, begun in 1760, whereby a Grand Jury at the Assizes could grant money to applicants who proposed to build roads or bridges from county funds, though later the tax was levelled on the baronies, whose people presumably saw and used the highways for which they had to pay. All main coach roads had a metalling of broken stones, 18-21 ft. wide, 8 in. deep at the centre and 5 in. at the sides with gravel borders, and roads between market towns had 15-18 ft. of screened gravel with 12-15 ft. on minor highways.[14] The turnpike roads had been difficult to maintain as the income from tolls was inadequate though some of the minor roads, developed before the presentment system, were well maintained. It seems that the quality of the roads differed from one area to another. Rev. John Wesley found the roads[15] 'wonderful' near Manorhamilton on 21 May 1789, but 'miserable' near Coleraine on 3 June, but perhaps the fact that 'the axletree of my chaise snapped in two' only a quarter of an hour after his departure upset him (he was then 86): in 1787 he gave an adverse view of Irish roads from Armagh.[16]

> We went on through horrible roads to Newry. I wonder any should be so stupid as to prefer the Irish roads to the English. The huge unbroken stones of which they are generally made, are enough to break any good carriage in pieces; no, there is nothing equal to good English gravel, both for horses, carriages, and travellers.

The Presentment Act ruled that no stones should be of more than 2½ in. in diameter but possibly this rule was not always observed.

Canals and river navigations appeared to offer great advantages to Ireland during the eighteenth century and much of the nineteenth for many writers, such as Sir Robert Kane in 1844, who hoped that the Shannon would become a great artery of commerce and that many more canals would be built. He also favoured the provision of roads and government-owned railways.[17] Of the canals the most remarkable was the Newry navigation, constructed between 1731 and 1742, the earliest man-made inland canal in the British Isles.[18] Eighteen miles long, the canal runs from a lock to the south of Newry to the upper Bann river at Whitecoat Point one mile south of Portadown, where the river is navigable into Lough Neagh. One aim was to carry coal from the Tyrone collieries around Coalisland, but the short canal from this mining area to Lough Neagh was not completed until 1787. Meanwhile the position of Newry had been strengthened by the completion of the Ship Canal, also the first in the British Isles, by 1769; this canal, 60 ft. wide and 12 ft. deep, could handle vessels of up to 120 tons and a lock was built at Warrenpoint to take larger vessels. Newry became a strong port serving much of the Ulster province and even for a time the effective rival of Belfast. The other and greater scheme of inland navigation was to link Dublin with the Barrow valley to Waterford and with the Shannon to Limerick. From 1759 several short stretches of canal were built around rapids in the Barrow river but slow progress was made with the Grand Canal.[19] From 1755 to 1779 only twelve miles was built and it took another twenty-five years to reach the Shannon in 1804: the canal reached Athy on the Barrow in 1791, Philipstown in 1798, and Tullamore in 1799. Branches were opened, with government aid, to Ballinasloe in 1828, Mountmellick in 1830 and Kilbeggan in 1835. The canal proved to be far more expensive than was forecast but in the pre-railway era it was thoroughly used for both passengers and freight. The Royal Canal,[20] which runs for 91 miles from the north side of Dublin, was constructed between 1789 and 1817 but passes through only two significant towns, Mullingar and Longford, and leads to the upper part of the Shannon valley. In never had more than a fraction of the trade of its rival and probably was unnecessary. Improvements in the Shannon made possible steam-ship services on the river with its spreading lakes and on the long estuary to Tarbet and Kilrush. Undoubtedly these canals helped to give prosperity to some of the inland towns but the ports were still the major centres as, economically, Ireland was dominated by its export of agricultural produce. The river navigations such as the Boyne to Navan, developed from 1782, or the Suir to Clonmel, provided with a towpath by a government grant of 1765, were commercially helpful to the towns they served and therefore to the people who patronised their markets: in the north the canal to Strabane,[21] opened in 1793, provided a similiar stimulus. Nevertheless industrial development was slight, for all the hopes of economic growth based on the discovery of minerals, especially coal, proved vain.[22] Only gradually, from the second half of the eighteenth century, were signs appearing of a new destiny for the north, part (only) of the province of Ulster as the domestic industry of linen became increasingly successful.[23] But through the eighteenth century the historic ports of Dublin, Waterford, Cork and Limerick remained major centres, though the growth in trade of Newry, Belfast and Londonderry was notable.

In general one may infer that the idea of a town as a centre of commerce, law, justice, charity and other expressions of social and political well-being was clearly developed by the eighteenth century. No town existed in isolation and therefore roads, supplemented by river navigations and canals, must be provided and adequately maintained (Figure 14). Only in the nineteenth century was this fully achieved, for beyond the civilised part of Ireland there was a 'wild west' difficult of access, where the inhabitants could not sell their surplus grain because they were too far from any market, so they used it for illicit distillation of spirits which reduced them to a state of happy, if demoralising, euphoria.[24] One witness to the Devon Commission in 1847 spoke of the moral dangers of an agricultural community cut off from its neighbours by the lack of roads. He enjoyed their home-made whiskey while condemning its prevalence. The building of Clifden in 1815 and Belmullet in 1822, on the far western coasts of Connaught, and of the roads to Galway and Ballina early in the nineteenth century was hailed as a triumph,[25] as the expression of a civilising mission that would bring financial profit with social advance to the people of the district, including the landlords. True to the ethos of the time, the Devon Commission of 1847 regarded the landlords as the men responsible for the care of the people.[26] Their main preoccupation was with the rural community, but they were equally responsible for the improvement of the towns and their markets. Some towns in the eighteenth and nineteenth century were embellished by the landlords: others were not.

The Eighteenth-century Town

Arthur Young, writing in 1778, said that within the previous thirty years Ireland had 'made as great an advance as could possibly be expected, perhaps greater than any other country in Europe'.[27] Since 1748 her linen exports had trebled and her general exports to Great Britain had more than doubled. He wished to see the development of industry in the towns,[28] for

> manufacturers become the best friends to agriculture . . . they animate the farmer's industry by giving him ready markets; until he is able, not only to supply them thoroughly, but . . . finds a surplus in his hands to convert into gold in the national balance . . . wealth pours in from the fabricks, which, spreading like a fertile stream over all the surrounding lands, renders them, comparatively speaking, so many gardens, the most pleasing spectacles of successful industry.

He viewed with dismay the concentration of the rural population of the north of Ireland on domestic spinning and weaving, for he wished to see

Figure 14: Roads in 1837
Though views on Irish roads were mixed, in general they covered the country
by the time the roads to the west were completed. The map is based on Plate I
in the Atlas which accompanied the *Record Report of the Railway Commissioners,
Ireland*, 1838, and first published in *Pre-Famine Ireland* (Manchester, 1957), p. 110.

a farming community that lived in the field rather than beside a loom and wanted the landlords to 'drive their weavers into towns' and 'steadily refuse to let an acre of land to any man that has a loom'. Arthur Young was probably, even certainly, a more acute observer than John Wesley[29] who, in July 1756, said that

> No sooner did we enter Ulster, that we observed the difference. The ground was cultivated just as in England, and the cottages not only neat, but with doors, chimneys and windows. Newry, the first town we came to, (allowing for its size), is built much after the manner of Liverpool.

A few days later he was in Belfast, 'the largest town in Ulster', which he found to be 'far cleaner and pleasanter' than Limerick, said to be of much the same size. Whether Young took a somewhat jaundiced view of the agriculture of Ulster is doubtful, though other and later travellers took a favourable view of 'the North' as the one area of Ireland showing real economic advance. But the renewed interest in 'perception' in our own day reveals, not for the first time, that people are likely to see what they want to see: Wesley was mainly concerned with the souls of men and Young with their crop rotations.

That many notable improvements were made in the towns of Ulster during the eighteenth century has been splendidly shown by Gilbert Camblin in *The Town in Ulster*.[30] There was no standard plan, as in many cases the actual form of a town had to be adjusted to local site conditions. Even in Belfast the curve of High Street marks the course of the river Farset, eventually covered over just as the channels between the islands of central Cork were to define the main streets. In Armagh roads were built on level land around the ancient Cathedral placed on a prominent hill, and the town square was so laid out that there was an unimpeded view of the east end of the Cathedral. At Newry, clearly expected to enter a prosperous phase once the customs house was transferred from Carlingford in 1727, long central streets follow the line of the river and the main street has three small squares instead of one great central space. But the more general aspiration was to have one impressive square, of which a fine example is that of Newtownards, laid out in 1770 with a handsome market house built some thirty years earlier and a new town hall beside it. A markedly different place was Cookstown, County Tyrone, laid out as one main tree-lined street 130 ft. wide and 1¼ miles long. Gradually all the frontages were taken up and the town was complete by 1832: to this day there has been little development of the town along the roads crossing the main street except near the railway station.

Many landlords of the time had the idea of making a stately town, and so also had the London Livery Companies who planted the county of Derry from 1610. Their main centre was Derry (Figure 12), said by Thomas Molyneux in 1708 to be 'a good, compact, well-built town with some newly-built houses of quality'.[31] Growth was slow, however, though quickened after a bridge was built across the Foyle in 1790. Some towns acquired their dignified appearance by the accretion of good buildings, while others are more homogenous. Lisburn,[32] for example, was splendidly rebuilt by Lord Conway at the beginning of the eighteenth century and described by Molyneux in 1708 as 'one of the beautifullest towns perhaps in the three kingdoms – all brick houses, slated . . . all new and almost finished, rising from the most terrible rubbish that can be imagined.' Several other new buildings were added during the eighteenth century and Lisburn continued to be a handsome and prosperous town. Of all the rebuilding during the eighteenth century none was more striking than the work of Dr Richard Robinson, Archbishop of Armagh[33] from 1767. With the help of famous architects of the day, he repaired the cathedral and replaced its shingle roof by one of slates, founded the Library and Observatory, a new palace and a school.[34] John Wesley, on his visit of 22 June 1778, was full of admiration.

> I took a walk to the Primate's . . . The house is neat and handsome, but not magnificent. The domain is beautifully laid out in meadow-ground, sprinkled with trees; on one side of which is a long hill, covered with a shrubbery, cut into serpentine walks. On each side of the shrubbery is a straight walk, commanding a beautiful prospect. Since this Primate came, the town wears another face. He has repaired, and beautifully, the Cathedral, built a row of neat houses for the Choral-Vicars, erected a public library, and an infirmary, procured the free-school to be rebuilt of the size of a little college, and a new-built horse-barrack, together with a considerable number of convenient and handsome houses; so that Armagh is at length rising out of its ruins into a large and populous city.

Handsome towns were no doubt a source of satisfaction to Ulstermen then as now, but their residents were naturally concerned mainly with making a living. The linen-spinning and weaving of the rural population, and also of some townspeople, depended on the markets, of which a vivid description is given by Arthur Young[35] (July 1776).

> The cambricks are sold early, and through the whole morning; but
> when the clock strikes eleven the drapers jump upon stone steadings,
> and the weavers instantly flock about them with their pieces: the
> bargains are not struck at a word, but there is a little altercation,
> whether the price shall be one-halfpenny or a penny a yard more or
> less, which appeared to me useless. The draper's clerk stands by him,
> and writes his master's name on the pieces he buys, with the price;
> and, giving it back to the seller, he goes to the draper's quarters, and
> waits his coming. At twelve it ends, then there is an hour for mea-
> suring the pieces, and paying the money . . . Three thousand pieces
> a week are sold here, at 35s. each on the average, or £5,250, and per
> annum £273,000.

Obviously these linen markets brought money to the towns and to the
bleach greens, which were normally in rural areas. In the eighteenth
century the linen trade was a contributor to the general economic life
of a town much as the sale of agricultural produce was in its retail
markets. That the profits made by some of the linen factors were a
basis for industrialisation was to be seen later. The export of linen was
mainly to London through Derry, Newry and Belfast: two-thirds was
sent from Belfast, a little from Derry and the rest from Newry.[36] At
this time Newry was 'exceedingly flourishing', according to Young. The
buildings were good and he was 'amazed' to see ships of 150 tons and
more in the canal to Lough Neagh. Apart from linen, the main exports
from Belfast were of agricultural produce, notably beef, butter and
pork to the West Indies and France, though as yet industry was represented mainly by curing establishments for beef and pork, and by the
refining of imported sugar. But the town was growing, and Young[37]
found it well built, of brick, with broad straight streets, with an estimated population of 15,000. The whole town belonged to Lord
Donegall, who was building an elegant assembly room over the
Exchange. From Belfast, as also from Derry, there was considerable
overseas emigration, but Young thought that those who went were
mainly the dissolute and idle ('no loss to the country'), a view not
generally held in the discussions of Irish emigration that have continued
to this day.[38]

    Turning southwards, the city that fascinated travellers was Cork. It
was the second city of Ireland until the nineteenth century, when it was
outshone by Belfast. Cork was a major trading town, having agricultural

industries such as the salting of beef, butter and pork, with an export of hides, tallow, soap and glue and — a major item — woollen yarn. Young[39] found the town thronged on a market day and added that it resembled a Dutch town, for 'there are many canals, in the streets, with quays before the houses'. Although there were some fine streets and houses, 'the old part of the town is very close and dirty'. Cork was a centre for trade with America and its provisions were bought not only for export to colonial areas and the West Indies, but also for consumption on naval and civilian boats. Its merchants had built up prosperous businesses which, in Young's view, could well have been expanded, but the pleasures of living in so delectable an environment, 'preference to anything I have seen in Ireland', perhaps inhibited progress. Why should it be, he asks, that there was no more export trade than in the reign of Charles II? Rev. John Wesley,[40] travelling though Ireland at much the same time as Arthur Young, records that on 28 April 1778 he preached at Cork on 'To abstain from fleshly desires' which he said was 'a necessary lesson in every place and nowhere more so than in Cork'.

Undoubtedly Cork was a regional centre in the eighteenth century, and Young, like many writers before and since, was fully aware of the richness of the Munster lowlands.[41] Domestic industry was well established, and wool was brought from the counties of Roscommon and Galway, combed into 24-ounce balls and spun into worsteds, then exported to Yarmouth for sale in Norwich or to Bristol. But three-quarters of the wool was exported as yarn, and half the wool in Ireland was combed in County Cork. Much of the domestic industry was handled by 'manufacturers' in the towns, and Young was informed that all the weavers 'are confined to towns, having no land but small gardens', though the working up of coarse wool as well as stocking knitting was widespread in the rural areas. Army clothing was made in Cork and various fabrics were made at Carrick-on-Suir,[42] 'one of the greatest manufacturing towns of Ireland' with 'three or four hundred employed': this is obviously not a large number. In some places the landlord was praised for his enterprise, notably at Blarney,[43] where Mr S.J. Jefferys had built no fewer than thirteen mills for the making of linen, cottons, stockings, woollens, leather and paper. Several hundred people were employed and the town, built from 1765 when there were only a couple of mud cabins, was 'built in a square, composed of a large handsome inn, and manufacturers' houses, all built of excellent stone, lime, and slate'. But there were always success stories and in general there was no sign of advance in the woollen industry,[44] though it was well established 'in the little towns of Doneraile, Mitchelstown,

Mallow, Kilworth, Kanturk and Newmarket', where there

> are clothiers, who buy up the wool, employ combers in their houses, who make considerable wages, and when combed, they have a day fixed for the poor to come and take it, in order to spin it into worsted, and pay them by the ball. . .

But the returns were very small. Linen-weaving still survived with Bandon as the main centre. As it happened, the linen industry declined to extinction, but the woollen and worsted industry still survives in Munster. Were the merchants of the towns missing chances of economic advancement? Young appears to have thought so, but perhaps like many Englishmen he misunderstood the nature of the Irish. Even in Mallow,[45] he thought, rich opportunities were being missed, for the spa water ('it resembles that of Bristol') was regarded as highly beneficial for many diseases. Social diversion was given by two assemblies each week. But the lodgings were expensive and 'miserably bad' and if only 'a double row of good lodgings were erected here, with public rooms, in an elegant style, Mallow would probably become a place for amusement, as well as for health'.

Waterford, like Cork, was a port firmly entrenched in the Atlantic trade, especially with Newfoundland, and many of its menfolk found employment as sailors.[46] The ships, Young notes, went out 'loaded with pork, beef, butter and some salt' and returned with varied cargoes, passengers, or even rum. Some of the young men went to work in Newfoundland for the summer months, and fishing was well developed around Waterford harbour, but only for local sale. Pig-rearing was notable in County Kilkenny and beef and butter were produced on the farms of the river valleys which converge in Waterford harbour. The town had a number of 'salt-houses' where the salt was boiled over lime kilns and there were two 'sugar-houses'. Other industrial activity included the manufacture of pots, kettles, weights and similar articles in common use and also the making of heavier goods, 'from anvils to anchors', partly for the ships. Then as now the situation of Waterford charmed visitors, for it stands on the south side of the river Suir opposite the steep cliff rising to 200 feet on the north side. Young was particularly impressed by the mile-long quay, even though he notes that there were 'only common hovels' beside it. The old medieval cathedral church had been demolished in 1773 and its successor, completed by 1776, was 'light and beautiful': any proposal to demolish a Gothic cathedral would be less favourably regarded now. Inland,

Clonmel,[47] also on the Suir and able to receive vessels of as much as
10 tons, had profited by the interest of the local landlord, Stephen
Moore of Marlfield, who had built a flour mill. He drew supplies of
grain from a radius of sixteen miles and sent most of the flour to
Dublin for biscuit-making, though some was made into bread at
Waterford. Rev. John Wesley, on his visit of 7 May 1756 found
Clonmel[48]

> the pleasantest town, beyond all comparison, which I have yet
> seen in Ireland. It has broad straight streets of well-built houses,
> which cross each other in the centre of the town. Close to the walls,
> on the south side, runs a broad, clear river. Beyond this rises a green
> and fruitful mountain and hangs over the town: the vale runs many
> miles both east and west, and is well cultivated throughout.

Eighteenth-century travellers were worried about political agitation in
the rural areas, and especially by the Whiteboys of County Tipperary
and elsewhere, but hoped that economic progress would remove the
propensity of the Irish to join secret societies bent on revolution. And
nobody appreciated more than Young the interlocking destiny of the
towns with the countryside, for the farmers could only advance by
selling produce for a market which in Ireland meant mainly an export
market. Yet there was much to discourage. In New Ross, for example,
with a fine harbour on the river Barrow capable of taking ships of 700
tons, trade was 'languid and trifling' and this was not only characteristic but also preventable. Young's watchword was 'EMPLOY, don't
hang them' for the Irish, if given property at a fair rent, would respect
it and if given 'the fruit of their labour' they would become, and
remain, 'laborious'.[49] These theories were in Young's estimation abundantly borne out in Mitchelstown, County Cork,[50] where from 1778-9
he was land agent to Lord Kingsborough, son of the Earl of Kingston.
It was not an inherently rich district such as the Golden Vale or the
lush pastoral valleys of Waterford and Cork, and it was crowded with
inhabitants, for the mud cabins of the poor swarmed with children and
also with pigs: 'pigs and children bask and roll about, and often
resemble one another so much, that it is necessary to look twice . . .
there are more pigs in Mitchelstown than human beings'. The cottiers
had dairy cows eventually sold at fairs but they could not keep all the
calves and even killed some two to three days old for veal. Poverty was
seen in the markets, 'for there is nothing too trifling to carry; a yard of
linen, a fleece of wool, a couple of chickens, will carry an unemployed

pair of hands ten miles.' And some men would walk as much as a dozen miles leading a lamb on a straw rope to be sold for 3s.6d. Lord Kingsborough, however, had progressive ideas. Fresh from the Grand Tour, 'just come from the gaieties of Italy, Paris and London', he dispensed with the hated middle man who charged the tenants more rent than he returned to the owner. He built a vast new mansion, offices, new farmhouses, so that

> Mitchelstown, till his Lordship made it the place of his residence, was a den of vagabonds, thieves, rioters and Whiteboys; but . . . now as orderly and peaceable as any other Irish town, much owing to this circumstances of building, and thereby employing such numbers of the people.

'Paternalism', to use a current pejorative word, it certainly was, but in 1776 and not 1976. What still survives is a well-laid-out small country town (Figure 15).

To the west, Limerick was a cheerful town in a cheerful countryside and its population, estimated to be 32,000 in 1776, gave it the status of the third town of Ireland. The older and central area was partly built on an island in the Shannon but the fine Georgian extension of Newtown Pery (Mr Pery was Speaker in the House of Commons), which is still an elegant feature of Limerick, had been built, together with docks, quays and a Custom House.[51] Excise duties had been increasing with the export of beef, pork, butter, hides and rape-seed and imports of rum, sugar, tobacco, wines, salt, coal and other commodities. Flour was sent to Dublin by road and butter was made in great quantities within a few miles of the town. A general indication of prosperity was given by the increase of carriages between the 1740s, when there were only four, and 1776, when there were about three hundred. Limerick was sufficiently large to have such entertainments as assemblies, concerts and plays. But the smaller towns were less fortunately placed, and Kilmallock,[52] a thriving town until it was damaged during the Cromwellian wars, was described by John Wesley as 'once a flourishing city, now a heap of ruins'. He also spoke of Clarecastle: 'What a contrast between Clare and Limerick! A little ruinous town! No inn that could afford us either meat, or drink, or comfortable lodging!' Fortunately the Army came to his help and gave him 'a tolerable lodging in the barracks'. Ennis was the county town with a Court House: Wesley spoke of it as 'a town consisting almost wholly of Papists, except a few Protestant gentlemen'. From Ennis Wesley

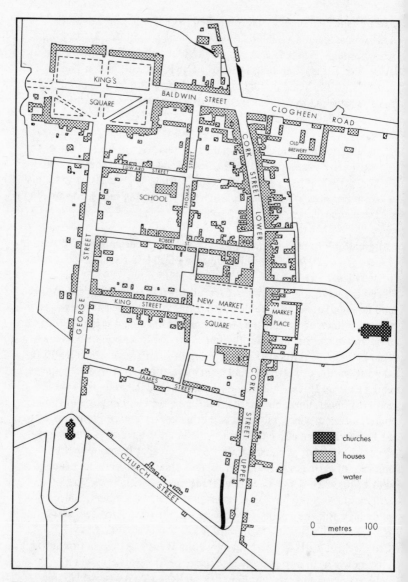

Figure 15: Mitchelstown in 1841
Built by the Kingston family, the town has all its houses on the street, a market square, the King's Square beside the gate of the demesne, an interesting mingling of straight and curved streets, a large Roman Catholic church and a smaller one for the Church of Ireland. The result was a stately country market town, similar to many others in Ireland. Originally published in *Irish Geography*, Vol. 2, No. 3 (1951), p. 107.

travelled north to Galway, and was surprised to find 'a fruitful and pleasant county', even though rocky in character. Galway[53] itself was redolent of history with high stone houses and it was 'encompassed with an old, bad wall . . . in no posture for defence, either towards the land or the sea'. Young was fascinated by the fishing of Galway and noted that there were over 200 boats based on the town, of which some forty or fifty were of several tons. All the fish was sold in Ireland, but some 3,000 tons a year of kelp, iodine made from burning seaweed, were exported annually. Efforts had been made to encourage flax-growing, with home spinning and weaving, in Galway and district with some success for a time,[54] but only for a time.

As a man dedicated to the improvement of land, Young hoped for much reclamation of the desolate wastes that lay in West Connaught. He was delighted to find an 'improver' in Lord Altamount at Westport, and was enchanted by the view from his house on the fringe of the town.[55] Those who have seen Clew Bay, with its numerous islands and its mountain background, including the massive Croaghpatrick, will understand Young's enthusiasm. Lord Altamount had built many new houses in the town and had established the linen industry by lending money to people to buy yarn for spinning: in time a bleach green and a mill were built. At Castlebar similar encouragement had been given to the linen industry by Lord Lucan, and the town was reported to be 'greatly rising from manufactures' with well-built houses. To the north Ballina, and the small village round a cathedral at Killala, were market centres; Ballina's famous salmon fishery gave seventy or eighty tons for salting as well as a large quantity sold fresh. In the markets at both Ballina and Killala some linen was almost always on sale, as well as general goods.[56] Fishing supported 150 boats on the bay of Killala and the Moy estuary. But to the west there was 'that wild and impenetrable tract of mountain and bog, the barony of Erris, in which 'there (was) not a post-house, market-town, or justice of peace'. It was inhabited in places but was beyond normal commerce until a road and the town of Belmullet were built later (p. 109). Sligo as a port was a useful stimulus to the surrounding area and Young quotes a local informant's comment that improvements in farming had begun about 1748 and continued with a steady increase in rents and production.[57]

Dublin as the unquestioned capital of Ireland surprised and delighted visitors in the eighteenth century.[58] Young, arriving in June 1776, found it 'much exceeded' his expectations for 'the public buildings are magnificent, very many of the streets regularly laid out, and exceedingly well built'. Elegance was seen in Trinity College, 'a beautiful building

and a numerous society' with a library, 'a very fine room, and well
filled'. Other handsome buildings included the Exchange and
Charlemont House. The superb setting of Dublin was well seen from
Lord Charlemont's villa at Marino (Clontarf), with 'a noble river
crowded with ships moving to and from the capital. On the other side
is a shore spotted with white buildings, and beyond it the hills of
Wicklow . . .' Young thought that the population might be as many as
200,000 but probably less; the 1804 computation was 167,900. That
there was great poverty was well known, for by the eighteenth century
the city had the crowded slums of the Liberties. But it was the
splendour of Dublin that attracted most attention from visitors and in
1758 John Wesley found the new front of Trinity College[59] 'exceeding
grand' though he thought that 'the whole square would be beautiful,
were not the windows too small, as every one will see, when the present
fashion is out of date'. On a later visit, in 1787, he toured the fine
apartments in the Parliament House[60] (now the Bank of Ireland)
opposite Trinity College: he noted that 'the House of Lords far exceeds
that at Westminster' and 'the House of Commons is a noble room
indeed . . . galleried all round for the convenience of the ladies'. Two
years earlier, 1785, Wesley had travelled on the Grand Canal from
Prosperous to Dublin by passenger boat,[61] 'a most elegant way of
travelling, little inferior to that of the Track-skuyts in Holland' and
preached (by request) to the passengers. Prosperous was 'a little town
begun five years ago' and 'about two thousand men, women, and
children' were employed. Houses had been built for workers, and
Prosperous was one example of commendable enterprise by the local
landowner, but in 1800 the enterprise failed.

Towns in the Central Lowland were of mixed quality but this
appearance was not necessarily indicative of this prosperity. Young,[62]
for example, found Mullingar 'a dirty ugly town' but he passed through
on a fair day when many cattle and horses were on sale. Tullamore[63]
was — in part at least — well built and had a fine Court House admired
by Wesley. In 1785 a fire balloon let off to celebrate the coming-of-age
of Lord Charleville burnt down much of the town but the rebuilding gave
it a new dignity of appearance. This was enhanced when the Grand
Canal reached the town in 1799 and an hotel, several warehouses, a
harbour and a dry dock were added. In 1804 the canal reached the
Shannon and Tullamore became a strong market centre, completely
superseding the old Tudor foundation of Philipstown which, like many
other towns founded both in Tudor and Anglo-Norman times, became
a mere village. Of the country towns, however, Kilkenny attracted a

great deal of attention from visitors: Wesley found it 'one of the pleasantest and most ancient cities in the kingdom' with its stately cathedral.[64] On the coast to the north of Dublin, Drogheda and Dundalk were both ports and major market centres. Drogheda was said by Wesley to be 'a large, handsome town . . . little inferior to Waterford', with crowded markets, well-used quays and boat traffic along the Boyne.[65] To Young, Dundalk[66] showed 'every mark of increasing wealth and prosperity', for it was 'full of new buildings' with 'many good stone and slate houses' and numerous bleach greens. While there were signs of advance in the prosperity of many towns, conspicuously seen in the buildings that still survive, poverty was rampant and the charitable instincts of the rich were amply engaged in providing hospitals, orphanages and similar institutions managed with varying degrees of compassion and efficiency. Perhaps Arthur Young was in one of his more optimistic moods when he wrote in 1779 that town expansion could only come through the increase of 'manufactures, commerce and luxury . . . other words for riches and employment'.[67] With such expansion, population increase would be helpful: without it dangerous. Young could not know that in the next 65 years, from 1780 to 1845, the population of Ireland would be doubled without the advance in industry that was seen in England, and that severe problems of population pressure were to be of dominating significance in the social history of nineteenth-century Ireland. Nor could he know that towns would grow in population by an influx of the destitute. Young's estimate of the population was 3,000,000 in 1778, but by 1841 it may well have been approaching 8,500,000.

The Nineteenth-century Town

Gazetteers, travellers' observations, census reports, Ordnance maps and other sources make it far easier to visualise the towns of the nineteenth century than those of an earlier time. A source of particular value is the census of 1841, which gives excellent statistical material for all settlements having more than twenty houses. Travellers' impressions, though subjective, are helpful and often entertaining, but the *Topographical Dictionary* of Samuel Lewis,[68] in 1837, a source that it was once fashionable to denigrate, gives contemporary information on towns that can be checked by reference to the new 6 inch to one mile Ordnance Survey maps issued from 1833 to 1846. All the surveying was completed before the famine, beginning in 1845, devastated the land and resulted in a greatly changed pattern of rural settlement. If Lewis said that a town had certain mills and factories, that can be

checked from the maps and the author, having done this, can assert that
Lewis is in general to be trusted. That his earlier history is suspect is
not of concern here.

If it is desired to establish an 'urban hierarchy' (detestable phrase),
the positions in 1841 were perfectly clear. There were only five towns
having more than 20,000 people, all of them ports. Dublin, the
unquestioned metropolis of a thousand years, had 232,726 people
living mainly within the two Circular Roads, though suburbs were
developing around the city, both inland and along the shores of Dublin
Bay (Figure 16). The city was the country's main port, mart and administrative centre, the focus of its road system and of its two major canals,
the Grand and the (less successful) Royal. It was obviously destined to
be the main railway centre, as the authors of the fascinating reports on
possible routes showed in 1936-8.[69] Waterford, on the Suir, was a port
drawing trade from a wide area in the south-east, by road and by boats
which used the Suir river and the canalised Barrow. Its quays were as
prominent a feature of its life as of its appearance and its 23,216
people lived mainly on the hillside gently rising southwards from the
river, as little land was available on the north side. Far greater in significance, however, was Cork,[70] with 80,720 people, with its commercial
heart on the level land, made into a single island from several around
while the river Lee flows in two channels. Valley sides rising to 200
feet on both sides provided fine sites for houses and public buildings
and some of the wealthier citizens lived outside the town on Cork
harbour which had a number of sea-bathing resorts. The main exports
were agricultural in origin, especially butter collected from the counties
of Cork, Limerick and Kerry, with beef, pork, bacon and hams. With
Cove (to become — for a time — Queenstown in 1848 as a commemora-
tion of Queen Victoria's visit) as an outport, Cork was firmly established
as a victualling centre for the British Navy and also derived profit from
supplying ships crossing the Atlantic. Agricultural industries were prominent, especially brewing, distilling and milling with bacon-curing, but
there were also factories for footwear, textiles, both woollen and
cotton, and a number of minor enterprises. Limerick[71] on the
Shannon, with 48,391 inhabitants, was even more dependent on
agricultural trade than Cork for virtually all its exports were of wheat,
flour, cattle, butter, pork and bacon, and its chief industries were
bacon-curing, flour-milling, brewing and distilling. Linen-weaving had
declined almost to extinction and many of the smaller industrial plants,
such as iron-founding and coopering, were obviously set up to meet
the needs of farmers. All of these four towns were Norse foundations

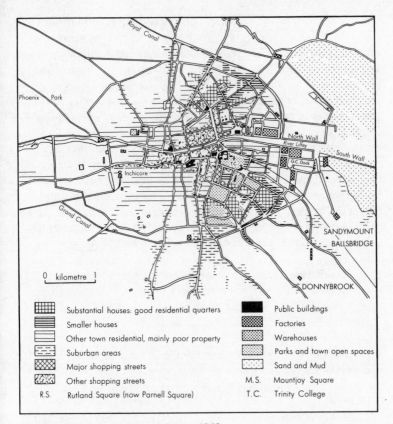

Substantial houses: good residential quarters
Smaller houses
Other town residential, mainly poor property
Suburban areas
Major shopping streets
Other shopping streets
R.S. Rutland Square (now Parnell Square)

Public buildings
Factories
Warehouses
Parks and town open spaces
Sand and Mud
M.S. Mountjoy Square
T.C. Trinity College

Figure 16: Town Land Use in Dublin c. 1840
The favoured areas were the Georgian quarters in the north-east and south-east of the city and the suburbs in the south side. To the west much of the property was crowded and so too were the streets near the quays beside the Liffey with some slums. The influence of the canals on the plan of the growing city is clear. First published in *Pre-Famine Ireland* (Manchester, 1957), p. 158.

and all were regarded by travellers with interest as they had many fine buildings and stately streets as well as warren-like slums.

But the town that called forth superlatives from visitors was Belfast,[72] with 75,308 people in 1841, already the country's second port as well as a rapidly growing industrial centre. Travellers recognised in Belfast the same spirit of enterprise that had made Liverpool, Manchester and other British towns great[73]; and they approved. Inglis thought that it was impossible that Cork, Limerick or Waterford could ever become like Belfast, for people in the southern cities were addicted to pleasure, which in Belfast was 'a very secondary consideration'. Harbour improvements, new docks and especially the cutting of a deep channel in the Lagan from 1839 all stengthened the maritime trade in agricultural produce, including pork and grain as well as linen. The transition from the domestic to the factory spinning and weaving of linen was a long process, but by 1841 there were over twenty flax-spinning mills in Belfast; and a variety of other industries, including tanning, paper manufacture, rope-making, iron and brass foundries, glass-making as well as brewing and distilling, were established. Many of these trades contributed to the success of shipbuilding.[74] Plenty of land was available for new enterprises in the Lagan estuary, and in time reclamation added excellent level sites for expansion. No single reason can be given for the industrial success of Belfast, but the commercial acumen of its people was considerable. Most of the travellers said that the town was growing fast. It had, said the Halls,[75]

> so much bustle . . . it is a new town, and has a new look. It is undoubtedly the healthiest manufacturing town in the Kingdom; although densely populated, there is far less wretchedness in its lands and alleys, and about its suburbs, than elsewhere in Ireland . . .[76]

Inglis thought that it was bound to flourish because so many of its inhabitants were of Scottish origin ('the character of the Scottish and the Irish is essentially different'), but then he was a Scot himself (Figure 17).

Only thirteen towns had between 10,000 and 20,000 people, and only five of these — Kilkenny, Carlow, Clonmel, Carrick-on-Suir, and Armagh — were inland centres. Mere size, however, meant little, for some places were full of unemployed and destitute people. Inglis found that both the woollen and carpet factories in Kilkenny[77] had failed and the Halls said that 'poverty had forced its way into nearly every cabin; and absolute starvation might be noted in many a form and face'. With 19,071 people, it was regarded as the chief inland town of Ireland and it remained a major market centre despite its industrial misfortunes. Even more depressing was the situation at Carrick-on-Suir (11,049) where the woollen trade had ceased and according to Inglis 'a constant deterioration had taken place in the condition of this town, and its neighbourhood, during the last ten years'.[78] This was visible in 'houses and shops shut up, and windows broken . . . [a] very poor and ragged population that lingered about the streets.' But, Clonmel (13,505) thirteen miles further on in the Suir Valley, was doing well.[79] Though it had lost its woollen industry, road and river transport met here and its warehouses were filled with grain,

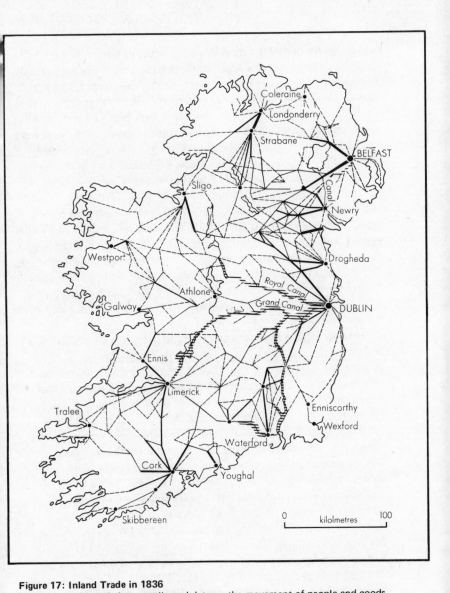

Figure 17: Inland Trade in 1836
The Railway Commissioners collected data on the movement of people and goods
along rivers, roads and canals and published their findings in a report illustrated by
a splendidly drawn 'flow' map. At the time the canals were prosperous and the
use of the Shannon was so notable that contemporary and later authors, like Sir
Robert Kane, expected it to become even greater. A clear distinction emerged
between the richer east and the poorer west, broadly definable by a line from
Derry to Cork. Based on Plate III in the Atlas which accompanied the *Second
Report of the Railway Commissioners, Ireland*. Ireland, 1838, and first published
in *Pre-Famine Ireland* (Manchester, 1957), p. 117.

butter and bacon to be carried by road or river to Waterford for shipping to Liverpool and Manchester. Bacon-curing, flour-milling and cotton-weaving (the last under the care of the Malcolmson family, a Quaker family who had built the factory at Portlaw) were all successful. Clonmel was the assize town for the South Riding of Tipperary and had a garrison. There too the headquarters of the Bianconi car services were established in 1815 and for thirty years, before the railways covered Ireland, they were extremely successful.[80] The last town in this group, Armagh (10,245) was relatively more important in the 1840s than later, for though a major road junction it was – perhaps fortunately – outshone by the growth of its neighbour Portadawn, which grew rapidly when the railways were built. Armagh[81] was a strong market in a fertile district with flour and corn mills, breweries, distilleries and tanneries: the tradition of fine building (see p. 112) had continued and both Inglis and the Halls found it a handsome town, with far fewer poor houses than in many others. This was confirmed by the 1841 census which in its remarkable analysis of housing showed that less than one-tenth of the houses were in the fourth or lowest (cabin) class.

That the eight other towns in this statistical group were all ports is indicative of the nature of the Irish economy in pre-famine times (Figure 18). In every case their limited prosperity depended on the export of agricultural produce and the import of fuel, raw materials and manufactured goods. All served extensive rural hinterlands and none had any marked signs of industrial growth. On the Foyle estuary Derry (15,196), much admired for its fine hill site and even compared with Edinburgh, showed definite signs of expansion for the Waterside suburb was growing on the east side of the river and houses were being built along roads leading from the walled town. Beyond the town, said Inglis, 'up river and down the estuary, the slopes and heights are adorned by handsome villas'.[82] Though some linen was exported it was still a domestic trade, and the main industries were flour-milling, brewing and distilling. The port served the entire Foyle basin with its various tributary valleys in the sperrin mountains to the east and the Donegal uplands to the west. Newry (11,792), a port depending on its Ship Canal and the inland waterway to Lough Neagh and Belfast, was the chief market centre for the area south of Lough Neagh, but drew its agricultural exports from a far wider area.[83] Its industries included two iron foundries for casting spades (made in a fascinating variety of shapes for different areas), flour-milling and distilling. Newry's two distilleries, however, failed to survive the total abstinence campaign so vigorously preached by Father Mathew in the 1840s. At Bessbrook, two

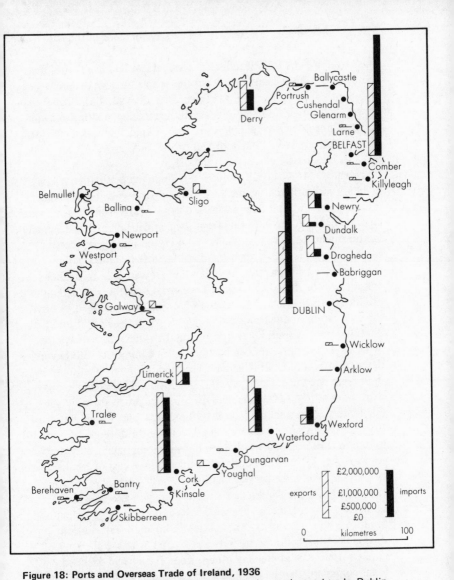

Figure 18: Ports and Overseas Trade of Ireland, 1936
For each port the thickness of the lines is in proportion to the total trade. Dublin had an excess of imports, like many capital cities, and Belfast, as a growing industrial centre, of exports, though in all the places shown agricultural exports were of major significance. Trade in the west was small and the dominance of a few ports was already clear. Of these, Dublin, Waterford and Cork were long-established centres with Belfast as the success story of the time. Newry's great days were over though Drogheda's hold on the trade of the rich hinterland, broadly the Boyne valley, was notable. Based on the map by H.D. Harness (which has a line shading of superb craftsmanship) in the Atlas which accompanied the *Second Report of the Railway Commissioners*, 1838 and first published in *Pre-Famine Ireland* (Manchester, 1957), p. 80.

miles from Newry, a linen mill and model village had been built, but though this provided some work for the people of Newry there were abundant signs of poverty in the town. Dundalk (10,782), smaller than Newry, had agricultural industries including milling, malting, brewing and distilling as well as tanning and iron-working.[84] It was the eighth port of Ireland, with only about half of the trade of Newry, and almost all of its exports were of agricultural origin.

Drogheda (16,261) had more export trade than either Newry or Dundalk and gathered the produce of the Boyne Valley by the much-criticised and difficult river navigation and by carts from an even wider area. Its flax mill was suffering from the competition of Dundee manu-facturers who made similar goods, but a cotton mill was successfully established in the 1830s; its other manufactures included leather and footwear, soap and candles, of which the last were sold throughout the counties of Meath and Cavan by carriers who brought back agricultural produce to its markets.[85] Drogheda's brewing even managed to survive the desiccating eloquence of Father Mathew and the Halls found that the town had 'an appearance of bustle and business' with quays that 'work as if they were trodden by the foot of commerce'. But beyond the main streets of what must have been (and still is) a handsome town there were wretched 'cabin suburbs' of considerable extent: in 1841 there were nearly 3,000 inhabited dwellings in Drogheda, of which one-tenth were substantial houses of more than nine rooms and one-fifth houses with five to nine rooms. Over one-third were cottages with two to four rooms, and another third were cabins having only one room. At Wexford (11,252), the only other town on the east of comparable size, [86] the main industry was malting the barley grown in the south-east, chiefly for the Dublin market, but there was also a distillery, breweries, tanyards and a rope works. Its exports were of agricultural produce with — like many other parts — corn and meal and flour as the major items, followed by butter and cows, with a wide range of imports. Here too, as in many other places, fishing had declined: Inglis comments that he thought it was a flourishing town as during two days he was never asked for alms, but there was a 'long poor suburb, chiefly inhabited by fishermen'. As in many other places two types of suburban growth could be seen, first, the large houses with large gardens or even grounds of the moneyed classes and, second, the huddle of the wretched cabins so characteristic of the fringes of the Irish towns.

On the west coast the three largest towns (apart from Limerick, p. 122) were Tralee (11,383), Galway (17,275) and Sligo (12,272).

Tralee[87] had been greatly improved by the local landowner, Sir Edward Denny, and was by far the most prosperous town in Kerry, though its 'ship canal' was still being constructed in 1838 and was not completed until twenty years later. It had a strong trade in grain for the wheat, oats and barley grown in the surrounding lowlands, including those of the Dingle peninsula, were collected here, partly for export. There was also a bacon factory as well as brewing and distilling. In Connaught, Galway[88] attracted the interest of numerous visitors, both for its antiquity and for its fishing community who occupied the district enclave known as the Claddagh. At the 1841 census 559 fishermen were recorded: they travelled along the coasts from Limerick to Sligo and their womenfolk made nets at home. The port trade was steadily increasing, chiefly in grain, meal and flour, but to a minor extent in bacon and hams. Markets twice a week were vigorously supported. There were several flour mills, but distilling was declining through the success of Father Mathew's total abstinence campaign. A number of industries had been established, including brewing, paper-making, iron-working, tanning and rope-making. Public buildings included a handsome workhouse built in 1815, a prison on the island on the site of the modern cathedral, a workhouse and several convents and monasteries, some of them associated with large schools. Some domestic spinning still survived and 150 people were recorded as so employed in the 1841 census. Sligo,[89] like Tralee and Galway, was a regional centre owing much to distance from any rival town of comparable size. Inglis described it as 'the chief mart of the northwest of Ireland', with no town of any note westward nearer than Ballina, eastward than Enniskillen, southward than Boyle, all about thirty miles away. 'Without a due consideration of the geographical situation of Sligo,' he observed, 'one might feel surprise at the very extensive warehouses of groceries, clothes, cottons, cutlery.' Ships of 12 feet draught could reach its port, which had more trade than Galway in 1836 when its exports, valued at £338,900, were divided almost equally between corn, meal and flour, and provisions, chiefly butter, pork and bacon. There was also a small export of linen yarn but this was nearly extinct, and industry was represented by four breweries, a distillery, several flour mills and a number of the small workshop industries then typical of major country towns, making soap, candles, tobacco, hats, ropes and cables. As well as its shops and wholesale houses, corn and butter markets, and five annual fairs, Sligo was the country's administrative centre with the usual gaol, courthouse, hospitals and an increasing number of convents.

Of smaller towns, 32 had 5,000 to 10,000 people and 137 had 1,500

to 5,000 people: in Connaught there were only four towns in the former
group and sixteen in the latter. In effect these were the ordinary market
centres of the countryside, including some of the smaller ports and a
very few places such as Killarney (7,127) and Mallow (6,851) that
derived some profits from the tourist trade. A number of towns having
fewer than 1,500 people were in effect market towns, especially
Connaught. The towns as a whole were reasonably well provided with
public transport, as shown in Figure 19, though this was not due to
any marked industrial development. The comment made by H.D.
Harness in 1838 excellently summarised the situation:[90]

> Her traffic is almost exclusively confined to the conveyance of
> articles to and from the ports. She has no great manufacturing in-
> land towns receiving a variety of materials from different ports, and
> returning their commodities in complicated streams for exportation,
> or consumption; with the exception of the trade occasioned by four
> collieries as yet of small importance, the linen and some cotton
> manufactures, there does not appear to be any transit worth of note,
> other than agricultural produce.

Before the famine as indeed afterwards, the actual size of a town gives
only a limited indication of its economic state. Travellers' comments
on the poverty are numerous: exact analyses scarcely exist. But *The
Times* reporter T.C. Foster, who toured Ireland in the autumn of 1845,
made many interesting comments before he became obsessed by a
controversy with Daniel O'Connell. For Bantry[91] a detailed analysis
was made of local employment. The town had 4,082 inhabitants in
1841, and presumably much the same number when Foster arrived on
14 November 1845. Fishing occupied 250 heads of families, shop-
keeping 'about 50' with another 50 working as butchers. There were
'20 nailers' and about 30 heads of families who were in a wide variety
of occupations: with 80 labourers, it seemed that 480 heads of families
had some means of livelihood. But there were also 120 families, about
800 people, 'without means of living', of whom perhaps 50 lived entirely by 'begging' while the rest, who might have employment now and
then, had a garden and a pig, and sold coral sand and seaweed from the
bay. This, says Foster,

> may account for the apparent wretchedness of the greater part of
> the town. Many of these poor people are ejected tenants . . . who
> resort to the town to seek a hovel, and such chance work as they

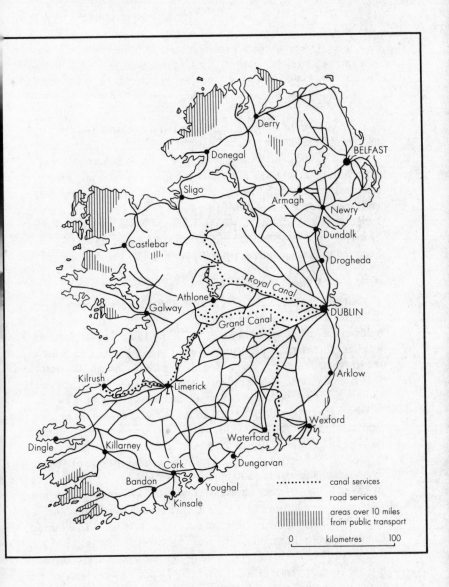

Map labels:

Derry, Donegal, BELFAST, Sligo, Armagh, Newry, Dundalk, Castlebar, Drogheda, Royal Canal, Athlone, Galway, Grand Canal, DUBLIN, Kilrush, Limerick, Arklow, Dingle, Killarney, Waterford, Wexford, Cork, Dungarvan, Bandon, Youghal, Kinsale

Legend:

•••••••••• canal services

—————— road services

||||||||| areas over 10 miles from public transport

0   kilometres   100

Figure 19: Canal and Road Services *c.* **1841**
Passenger boats on the canals, the Shannon and its estuary to Kilrush with various coach services and the 'cars' run by the Bianconi organisation from 1815 gave Ireland a reasonably adequate public transport service for the time, though some areas in the extreme west had no service within ten miles. The data was drawn from the *Second Report of the Railway Commissioners*, 1838, App. B, pp. 33-49 and R. Kane, *Industrial Resources of Ireland* (Dublin, 1845), pp. 331-5. The map was first published in *Pre-Famine Ireland* (Manchester, 1957), p. 112.

can get. Others of them 'squat' on some rocky uncultivated patch, contrive a wretched cabin to shelter themselves, and on their backs carry bog-earth from some exhausted bog to make a surface on the rock, and grow potatoes on which to exist.

He then goes on to compare Bantry unfavourably with Torquay, which had 'handsome villas . . . taste . . . diffused wealth . . . thriving activity . . . order . . . cleanliness'. In Bantry (in a far more beautiful setting than Torquay) there was 'not a decent building in the town' except for the courthouse, the church and the hotel, the streets were unpaved, unflagged and filthy and four-fifths of the people lived in 'mud hovels', such as you see in the country'. At this point Foster may be left, for he begins another of those sermons on 'hard persevering work' exported in large quantities from Britain to Ireland at the time.

After the Famine

That the famine was a catharsis of Irish history needs no emphasis. From 1845 there was a general decline in population from about 8½ million (8,175,124 in 1841) to 4,458,775 by 1901. The immediate loss was more than 20 per cent between 1845 and 1851, but many of the towns had more people in 1851 than in 1841, though this was due to the number who sought refuge in the workhouses, in hospitals and various charitable institutions. The inhumanity of the Poor Law has been too adequately documented, in Ireland as in Britain, to need emphasis here. At the 1841 census only 34,000 people were returned as builders and of these, 10,814 were employed by the Poor Law Commissioners. The Poor Law Unions were defined by the end of 1841 and in all except a few of the 130 unions the workhouses were opened by the end of 1845.[92] Built in what was called 'Domestic Gothic' they were austere but handsome additions to the towns (externally) though in some towns they held an incredibly large number of persons.[93] In Westport, County Mayo, for example, there were 6,410 inhabitants in 1841 and 8,229 in 1851, of whom 2,991 were in the new workhouse completed in 1845. In Skibbereen, County Cork, 2,717 people were inmates of the union and in Tralee almost twice as many. The Limerick union had space for 6,000 people and even in the relatively prosperous town of Dundalk hailed by many visitors as the 'gateway to the North', there were almost a thousand. The apparent increase in the urban population shown by comparing the figures for 1841 and 1851 is therefore misleading: far more perspicacious is the comment made in the splendid *General Report* of the 1926 census,[94] that in the Twenty-six Counties

that statistically 'the smaller the town, the worse it fares'. From 1841
to 1881, despite increases to 1851 in most towns, 11 towns of over
10,000 or more declined by 12 per cent, 26 of 5,000 to 10,000 by
25 per cent and 32 of 3,000 to 5,000 by 27 per cent, and the decline
was still continuing after 1891; for example, Westport had 6,410 people
in 1841, 8,229 in 1851, 4,070 in 1891 and only 3,488 in 1901. Within
the area that eventually became the Republic, the towns could not
absorb their own natural increase of population, still less the rural mi-
grants, and even Dublin grew only slowly. A table in the 1926 census
shows that the area that became most of Dublin and Dun Laoghaire
had 285,099 people in 1841 and 375,135 in 1901: three outlying
villages that later became suburbs, Terenure, Dalkey and Howth, were
growing but they had only 7,478 people in 1901 compared to 4,322
in 1841.

Only in the Ulster province, 'the north' to use the colloquial Irish
term, was there any real sign of economic growth. Those travellers who
had enthused on the economic vitality possessed by Belfast were justi-
fied by its rapid spread during the second half of the nineteenth
century. By 1901, it had 349,180 inhabitants, or 374,602 with its
immediate neighbours, Bangor, Holywood, Carrickfergus and Lisburn.
Beyond the obvious fact that Belfast had become as large as Dublin lies
the industrial success of shipbuilding and the linen industry. Within the
six counties that became Northern Ireland,[95] towns of 15,000 and over
had 35 per cent of the population by 1891, though the only towns
having more than 10,000 people, apart from Lisburn (12,250), were
Newry (12,961) and Bangor (11,429) and notably Derry (33,200).
And of these Derry had shown the most vigorous growth within the
previous fifty years, for it had become the centre of a shirt-making
industry that was located both in factories and in the homes of a wide
district, especially in County Donegal; it had passenger services to
British ports and an extensive shipping trade, some of it of people and
goods to and from America, and a small, but only intermittently successful shipbuilding yard as well as various other industries. Above all, it
was a regional capital for the north-west of Ireland. Lisburn and Lurgan
were growing towns sharing in the economic advance of Belfast and
district, and Newtonards had become a well-established, if small, industrial market town having 9,197 inhabitants by 1891. Even more
marked were the growth of Ballymena (5,152 people in 1841, 9,420 in
1891 and 10,886 in 1901) famed for its successful industries and
strongly Scottish sympathies. It was well provided with railway services,
and so too was Portadown, which became a major junction on the main

line between Belfast and Dublin. It had 2,505 people in 1841 and grew continuously (8,430 in 1891 and 10,092 in 1901) while its stately neighbour Armagh, eleven miles away, on a branch line built by 1848, remained a market town and residential centre, with its cathedrals and a famed observatory. Had the main line been taken through Navan (Co. Meath) and Armagh, as the Railway Commissioners[96] proposed, Armagh might have experienced the pulsating industrial growth of Portadown. Equally, Newry might have been more successful had the main line gone through it instead of on a ridge to the west of the town. Steadily its port declined through the competition of Belfast, successfully strengthening its dominance and centrality year by year. The towns of east Ulster profited by industrial growth while in the west Derry, seventy miles from Belfast, became what its founders of the seventeenth century hoped it might be, the major town of the north-west.

Hopes for a future brighter than the past were characteristic of Ireland at the end of the nineteenth century. But was it remarkable that the Handbook,[97] in fact a volume of over 500 pages, issued by the Department of Agriculture and Technical Instruction in 1902 should devote most of its space to agriculture? Most of the industries were based on agriculture and even the linen and the shirt industries of the north had developed from domestic crafts primarily in rural areas. Only the shipbuilding of Belfast, relying for its prosperity on imported raw materials, appeared to belong to the newer large-scale industrial development so characteristic of the time. There alone was something that could stand in rivalry beside the yards of Clydeside or the Tyne, an enterprise, known especially for its transatlantic ocean liners, throughout the world. The linen mills and other textile factories brought prosperity to numerous country towns, but all of them remained comparatively small and no major conurbation developed. Two Irish cities, so vastly different in their history and appearance, Dublin and Belfast, a hundred miles apart, had become the country's major centres and regional capitals. Then came the old Norse centres, Waterford in the south-east, Cork in the south-west, and Limerick on the Shannon, all static rather than growing. Other lesser regional capitals of the west were Galway and Sligo, and — larger than either by 1,900 — Derry on the Foyle. One thing had not changed, for all these places are ports. Inland there was the agricultural heart of the nation, generally sprinkled with towns about ten miles apart of which a few, especially in the north, had successful industries. And it was the difference between the industrial life of the north, with Belfast as its dominant centre, and the rest of Ireland with Dublin as its capital of a thousand years that, interpenetrating with a mass of social, religious and political attitudes, was to become a problem testing the sagacity of statesmen in the twentieth century.

Notes

1. Quoted in E.M. MacLeaght *Irish Life in the Seventeenth Century* (Cork and Oxford, 1950), pp. 226-7.
2. C.E.Maxwell, *Dublin under the Georges* (London, 1936); *Country and Town in Ireland under the Georges* (London, 1940).
3. D.A. Chart, *Ireland from the Union to Catholic Emancipation* (London, 1910), pp. 296-7, 300.
4. MacLysaght, op. cit., in note 1, pp. 183, 190.
5. Ibid., pp. 183, 189-90; D.J. Owen, *History of Belfast* (Belfast and London, 1921), p. 90.
6. T.W. Freeman, *Pre-Famine Ireland* (Manchester, 1957), pp. 33-5. The markets and fairs of Ireland are fully treated in *Report of the fairs and markets of Ireland*, 1853. Paul. P., 1852-3, Vol. XLI, Sess. No. 1674, p. 79.
7. G. Sjoberg, *The Pre-Industrial City* (Glencoe, 1960).
8. John Dunton's letters (in the Bodleian Library, Oxford, are printed in MacLysaght, op. cit., in Note 1, pp. 320-99. (on Galway, p. 328). A study of John Dunton is given in C.E. Maxwell, *The Stranger in Ireland* (London, 1954), pp. 118-24, where he is described as 'certainly an eccentric and towards the end of his life at any rate more than a little mad'.
9. W.M. Thackeray, *An Irish Sketch Book* (London, 1842), p. 219. He and several other travellers are discussed in Maxwell, op. cit., in note 8.
10. T.W. Freeman, *Geography and Regional Administration* (London, 1968), pp. 66-72.
11. T.W. Freeman, *Pre-Famine Ireland* (Manchester, 1957), table on p. 27.
12. *Report of the Commissioners appointed to take the Census of Ireland for the year 1841* (Dublin, for HMSO, 1843), p. viii.
13. A.W. Hutton (ed.), *Arthur Young's Tour in Ireland (1776-1779)* (London, 1892), Vol. II, p. 77.
14. Freeman, op. cit., in note 11, pp. 109, 111.
15. *The Journal of the Rev. John Wesley A.M. in 4 volumes,* Everyman edition (London, n.d.) Vol. 4, pp. 471, 474.
16. Wesley, op. cit., in note 15, Vol. 4, p. 395.
17. R. Kane, *Industrial Resources of Ireland* (Dublin and London, 1844), pp. 344-90. Sir Robert Kane's book went into a second edition in 1845.
18. W.A. McCutcheon, 'The Newry Navigation: the earliest inland canal in the British Isles', *Geographl. J.*, Vol. 129 (1963), pp. 466-80. See also A. Marmion, *The ancient and modern history of the maritime ports of Ireland* (London, 1856), pp. 123-4, 309-13, and W.A. McCutcheon, *The Canals of the North of Ireland* (Dawlish and London, 1965), pp. 17-39.
19. A Marmion, op. cit., in note 18, pp. 117-18; H. Phillips, 'The Grand Canal', *Journal of the Kildare Archaeological Society*, Vol. IX (Dublin 1918-22), pp. 434-6 and Vol. X (1922-8), pp. 3-28; C.E. Maxwell, *Country and Town in Ireland under the Georges* (London, 1940), pp. 313-22; T.W. Freeman, *Pre-Famine Ireland* (Manchester, 1957), pp.116-21; V.T.H. and D.R. Delany, *The Canals of the South of Ireland* (Newton Abbot, 1966), pp. 26-89.
20. Marmion, op. cit., pp. 121-2; Delany, op. cit., in note 19, pp. 77-91.

21. T.W. Freeman, op. cit., in note 19, p. 124.
22. Ibid., pp. 94-106, for a discussion of mineral resources in Ireland, with comment on Sir Robert Kane (see note 17) who took an optimistic view of the economic prospects. But as geological surveys developed it became clear that they were not as rich as earlier indications suggested and in 1885 Kane said that 'the Famine made such a profound alteration . . ., in the condition of the people that the subject of industry fell out of view.'
23. For a comprehensive study, see C.Gill, *The Rise of the Irish Linen Industry* (Oxford, 1925).
24. *Digest of evidence taken before H.M. Commissioners of Inquiry into the State of the Law and Practice in respect to the Occupation of Land in Ireland, 1847, Part I;* pp. v-702 (Dublin, 1847), Part II, pp. 703-1172 (Dublin, 1848). See evidence of 'John Fetherston, Esq.' on an area 'in the neighbourhood of Woodford, Co. Galway,' pp. 673-4. See also Kane, op. cit. (note 17, pp. 344-9.
25. *Devon Digest* (note 24), pp. 152-3, 680-1: Kane, op. cit. (note 17), pp. 344-50.
26. *Devon Digest,* esp. pp. 1025-35. The view that the landlords could make or break rural Ireland suffuses the report.
27. Young (see note 13), Vol. 2, pp. 258-9.
28. Op. cit., Vol. 2, p. 214.
29. Wesley (note 15), Vol. I, p. 346.
30. S. Camblin, *The Town in Ulster* (Belfast, 1951). For Belfast, see pp. 79-81, for Armagh 82-3, 92-3, and Newry, 76-7. See also C.E. Maxwell, *Country and Town in Ireland under the Georges* (London, 1940), especially Chapter 5 on 'The Provincial Towns'.
31. Camblin, op. cit., p. 87.
32. Ibid., p. 92.
33. Ibid., pp. 92-3.
34. Wesley, op. cit. (note 15), Vol. 4. p. 132.
35. Young, op. cit. (note 13), Vol. I, pp. 128-9.
36. Ibid., Vol. I, p. 144.
37. Ibid., Vol. I, p. 144.
38. Ibid., Vol. I, pp. 144-5.
39. Ibid., Vol. I, pp. 332-4.
40. Wesley, op. cit., (note 15), Vol. 4, p. 122.
41. Young, op. cit. (note 13), Vol. I, pp. 299-308.
42. Ibid., Vol. I, p. 402.
43. Ibid., Vol. I, pp. 312-13.
44. Ibid., Vol. I, p. 299.
45. Ibid., Vol. I, pp.308-9.
46. Ibid., Vol. I, pp. 406-8
47. Ibid., Vol. I, pp. 394-7.
48. Wesley, op. cit. (note 15), Vol. 2, p. 331.
49. Young, op. cit., (note 13), Vol. I, pp. 81, 399.
50. Ibid., Vol. I, pp. 458-64.
51. Ibid., Vol. I, pp. 292-5.
52. Wesley, op. cit. (note 15), Vol. I, p. 150, Vol. 3, p. 502; C.E. Maxwell, *Country and Town in Ireland under the Georges* (London, 1940), pp. 227-8, with illustration of *c.* 1820.
53. Wesley, op. cit., Vol. 2, p. 340.
54. Young, op. cit. (note 13), Vol. I, p. 276-7.
55. Ibid., Vol. I, pp. 250-8.
56. Ibid., Vol. I, pp. 245-7.

57. Ibid., Vol. I, pp. 240-1.

58. Ibid., Vol. I, pp. 17-21.

59. Wesley, op. cit. (note 15), Vol. 2, p. 407.

60. Ibid., Vol. 4, p. 397.

61. Ibid., Vol. 4, pp. 310, 325.

62. Young, op. cit. (note 13), Vol. I, p. 61.

63. Ibid., Vol. I, p. 62; T.W. Freeman, 'Tullamore and its environs', *Ir. Geog.*, Vol. 1, 1944-8, pp. 133-50. Wesley in 1789 mentioned 'the beautiful new court house' at Tullamore.

64. Wesley, op. cit. (note 15), Vol. 3, p. 101.

65. Ibid., Vol. 4, p. 324.

66. Young, op. cit. (note 13), Vol. I, p. 115.

67. Ibid., Vol. 2, pp. 253-4, 258-9.

68. The denigration of Samuel Lewis' work apparently began with a review in the *Dublin University Magazine*, Vol. 12, (1838), pp. 226-32, for even the entry in the *Dictionary of National Biography* misrepresents its tone. The original review is verbose but generally favourable: see T.W. Freeman, *Pre-Famine Ireland* (Manchester, 1957), p. 315, or – better still – the original review.

69. *Second Report of the Commissioners appointed to consider and recommend a general system of railways for Ireland* (Dublin, 1838) *Parl.P.*, Vol. 35, 1837-8, H.C. Session No. 145.

70. S. Lewis, *A topographical Dictionary of Ireland* (London, 1837), Vol. 2, pp. 687-90; H.D. Inglis, *A Tour throughout Ireland in the Spring, Summer and Autumn of 1834* (London, 1835), Vol. 1, pp. 60-7.

71. Lewis, op. cit. (note 70), Vol. 1, pp. 408-20; Inglis, op. cit. (note 70), Vol. 1, pp. 182-91; A. Marmion, *The Ancient and Modern History of the Maritime Ports of Ireland* (London, 1856), pp. 519-49.

72. Especially in Mr and Mrs S.C. Hall, *Ireland, its Scenery, Character etc.*, 3 vols. (London, 1841-3), Vol. 3, pp. 52-100; on the industrial history see E.R.R. Green, *The Lagan Valley, 1800-1850,* (London, 1949).

73. Inglis, op. cit. (note 70), Vol. 2, pp. 249-71.

74. T.W. Freeman, *Pre-Famine Ireland* (Manchester, 1957), p. 275.

75. Hale, op. cit. (note 72), Vol. 3, p. 53.

76. Inglis, op. cit. (note 70), Vol. 2, p. 251.

77. Inglis, ibid., Vol. 1, pp. 90-2; Hale, op. cit. (note 72), Vol. 2, p. 18.

78. Inglis, ibid., Vol. 1, pp. 72, 73.

79. Ibid., Vol. 1, pp. 130-5; Lewis, op. cit. (note 70), Vol. 1, pp. 369-71; Hall, op. cit., Vol. 2, p. 70.

80. On the Bianconi services, see Hall, op. cit., Vol. 2, pp. 76-9, and Inglis, op. cit., Vol. 1, pp. 52-6, for interesting contemporary accounts; it is treated as part of the general transport situation in Freeman, op. cit., pp. 107-27.

81. Freeman, ibid. pp. 285-6.

82. Ibid., pp. 293-4.

83. Ibid., pp. 284-5.

84. Ibid., p. 174.

85. Ibid., pp. 172-3. Earlier, Wesley spoke of Drogheda as 'this turbulent town' in op. cit. (note 15), Vol. 4, p. 395; the Halls took a favourable view, see op. cit. (note 72), Vol. 2, p. 424. But the 1841 census shows that there were 1,062 'cabins' in the town (2,995 inhabited houses).

86. Many contemporary writers visited Wexford. See Inglis, op. cit., (note 70), Vol. 1, pp. 43-6; Hall, op. cit. (note 72), Vol. 2, pp. 171-3 and G.L. Smyth, *Ireland Historical and Statistical*, Vol. 3 (London, 1849), p. 305. The town is also treated in Marmion, op. cit. (note 71), pp. 597-602. In the mid-nine-

teenth century the countryside to the west of the town (the baronies of
Forth and Bargy) was renowned for its fertility.

87. Inglis, op. cit. (note 70), Vol. 1, pp. 252-63.

88. Ibid., Vol. 1, pp. 22-34.

89. Ibid., pp. 122-5, 129-31. The port statistics for 1836 for the town are given
in the government report listed in note 69.

90. The comment by H.D. Harness also appears in the report in note 69,
Appendix No. III, p. 42.

91. T.C. Foster, *Letters on the condition of the people of Ireland* (London,
1847), pp. 401-3.

92. G. Nicholls, *A History of the Irish Poor Law* (London, 1856) in the best
source. See also Marmion, op. cit. (note 71), pp. 159-62, 625-6. Nicholls
shows that the number of persons received into workhouses was 417,000
in 1847, rising to 932,000 in 1849 but then diminishing to 505,000 by
1852. In 1848 and 1849 some form of relief was given to over 2,000,000
persons annually but though the effects of the famine lasted for several years,
by 1853 the number assisted had declined sharply. The number resident in
workhouses was 86,000 in 1846 rising to 155,000 in 1850 and then decreasing to 80,000 in 1853 and 67,000 in 1854 (on 29 September). As some
unions were excessively large, rearrangements in 1848 increased their
number to 163. For several years the workhouses were seriously overcrowded: see T.P. O'Neill on 'Poor law relief 1847-52', in R.D. Edwards
and T.D. Williams (eds.), *The Great Famine: Studies in Irish History*
(Dublin, 1956), pp. 244- 54.

93. Marmion, ibid., pp. 443, 501, 514.

94. *Saorstat Eireann, Census of Population 1926* (Dublin, 1934), Vol. 10,
pp. 13, 14 and 15-16 (tables of town population from 1841-1926).

95. T.W. Freeman, *Ireland: a general and regional geography* (London, 4th ed.,
1972), pp. 141-3, 145 for a survey of the population of Northern Ireland.

96. Freeman, op. cit., pp. 239-40; L. Murray, *The Great Northern Railway*
(Ireland) (Dublin, 1944), for an account of the controversies mentioned.
The original scheme for Irish railways is treated in the government report
listed in note 69.

97. W.P. Coyne (ed.), *Ireland, Industrial and Agricultural* (Dublin, 1902),
was based on a handbook issued for the Glasgow International Exhibition
of 1901 but was 'practically a new book' with '250 pages of fresh matter'
according to the preface. It is an excellent survey of economic conditions
at the turn of the century.

NOTES ON CONTRIBUTORS

R.A. Butlin is Senior Lecturer in Geography, Queen Mary College, University of London.

B.H. Graham is Senior Lecturer in Geography, School of Environmental Science, Ulster College, The Northern Ireland Polytechnic.

T.W. Freeman is Professor of Geography, University of Manchester.